Lab Manual for
CWNA Guide to Wireless LANs, Second Edition

Kelly Cannon

COURSE TECHNOLOGY
CENGAGE Learning

Australia • Brazil • Japan • Korea • Mexico • Singapore • Spain • United Kingdom • United States

COURSE TECHNOLOGY
CENGAGE Learning

Lab Manual for CWNA Guide to Wireless LANs, Second Edition
by Kelly Cannon

Managing Editor: William Pitkin III

Production Editor: Susan Forsyth

Product Marketing Manager: Gayathri Baskaran

Editorial Assistant: Jennifer Smith

Text Design: GEX Publishing Services

Product Manager: Amy M. Lyon

Technical Editor: John Bosco

Manufacturing Coordinator: Melissa Hulse

Cover Design: Abby Scholz

Compositor: GEX Publishing Services

Developmental Editor: Dan Seiter

Quality Assurance Coordinator: Christian Kunciw

Associate Product Manager: Sarah Santoro

For product information and technology assistance, contact us at
Cengage Learning Customer & Sales Support, 1-800-354-9706

For permission to use material from this text or product, submit all requests online at **cengage.com/permissions**
Further permission questions can be emailed to
permissionrequest@cengage.com

ISBN-13: 978-14188-3538-5
ISBN-10: 1-4188-3538-2

Course Technology
25 Thomson Place
Boston, Massachusetts, 02210
USA

Cengage Learning is a leading provider of customized learning solutions with office locations around the globe, including Singapore, the United Kingdom, Australia, Mexico, Brazil, and Japan. Locate your local office at: **international.cengage.com/region**

Cengage Learning products are represented in Canada by Nelson Education, Ltd.

Disclaimer: Course Technology reserves the right to revise this publication and make changes from time to time in its content without notice.

For your lifelong learning solutions, visit **course.cengage.com**

Purchase any of our products at your local college store or at our preferred online store **www.ichapters.com**

Printed in Canada
5 6 7 8 9 WC 11 10

TABLE OF CONTENTS

INTRODUCTION

Hands-on learning is the best way to master the wireless networking skills necessary for Planet3's Certified Wireless Network Administrator (CWNA) exam and a career in wireless networking. This book contains dozens of hands-on exercises that apply fundamental wireless networking concepts as they would be applied in the real world. In addition, each chapter offers multiple review questions to reinforce your mastery of wireless networking concepts. The organization of this manual follows the same organization as Course Technology's *CWNA Guide to Wireless LANs, Second Edition*, and using the two together will provide an effective learning experience. This book is suitable for use in a beginning or intermediate wireless networking course. As a prerequisite, students should be familiar with the basic operation of traditional wired networks.

FEATURES

To ensure a successful experience for instructors and students alike, this book includes the following features:

- **CWNA Certification Objectives** — Each chapter lists the relevant objectives from Planet3's CWNA Certification Exam.

- **Lab Objectives** — Every lab has a discussion of relevant wireless concepts and a description of learning objectives.

- **Materials Required** — Every lab includes information on hardware, software, and other materials you will need to complete the lab.

- **Completion Times** — Every lab has an estimated completion time, so that you can plan your activities more accurately.

- **Step-by-Step Instructions** — Logical and precise instructions, including activity questions, guide you through the hands-on activities in each lab.

- **Review Questions** — Five review questions at the end of each lab help reinforce concepts presented in the lab.

- **Software CD:** This lab manual comes with a CD that includes free software demo packages for use with the labs in this lab manual. Four software companies have graciously agreed to allow us to include their products with our lab manual: NetStumbler (*www.netstumbler.com*), AiroPeek SE from WildPackets, Inc. (*www.wildpackets.com*), AirMagnet (*www.airmagnet.com*), and Putty.exe (*www.chiark.greenend.org.uk/~sgtatham/putty/download.html*). You can check these Web sites for product information and updates. Additional software demos or freeware (besides those on the CD) are also used in this lab manual, and can be downloaded before you begin. A full list of the software and hardware used in the lab manual is included in Appendix A.

Note for instructors: Answers to activity and review questions as well as important lab tips are available on the Course Technology Web site at www.course.com/irc/. Search on this book's ISBN, 1-4188-3538-2, or on the ISBN for the core text, 0-619-21579-8.

Lab Setup Requirements

Most labs in this manual require laptops running Windows XP with Service Pack 2. The wireless equipment includes Cisco 1200 series access points and Cisco Aironet a/b/g cardbus adapters. Some labs require Linksys Wireless-G routers. See Appendix A for detailed lab setup instructions, including hardware requirements, student team setup, laptop preparation, additional software requirements, access point preparation, and naming conventions. We highly recommend that you read Appendix A before purchasing any hardware.

ACKNOWLEDGMENTS

Thanks to Course Technology for continuing to involve me in the world of academic publishing. Specifically, I want to thank Will Pitkin, Amy Lyon, and Susan Forsyth. I also thank Dan Seiter, who is a superb Developmental Editor, and John Bosco, who did a great job stepping through the labs. Thanks also to Chris Kunciw, Burt LaFontaine, and Shawn Day for making sure the labs worked in their final form. In addition, I want to thank the team of peer reviewers who evaluated each chapter and provided helpful suggestions and contributions:

Ijaz Awan	Savannah State University
Shannon Beasley	Central Georgia Technical College
Bruce Hartpence	Rochester Institute of Technology
Michael Moats	Hillsborough Community College

In addition, the Fall 2004 and Spring 2005 wireless administration students at Piedmont Virginia Community College played a crucial role in the development of this lab manual. Because of these 40 students, I was confident that the labs I created would work for others.

Finally, I want to thank my wonderful family: Jim, Veronica, and Adrienne, and my parents, who had the foresight to bring me to the greatest country in the world, where I continue to be blessed with opportunities.

IT'S A WIRELESS WORLD

Labs included in this chapter

➤ Lab 1.1 Defining Common Wireless Terms
➤ Lab 1.2 Comparing Wireless Systems to Wired Systems
➤ Lab 1.3 Exploring the Differences Between Bluetooth and Wi-Fi

---

CWNA Exam Objectives	
Objective	**Lab**
Identify the technology roles for which wireless LAN technology is an appropriate technology application	1.1
Identify, apply, and comprehend the differences between wireless LAN standards	1.3
Understand the roles of organizations in providing direction and accountability with the wireless LAN industry	1.3
Not all labs map to a certification objective; however, they contain information that will be beneficial to your professional development.	

Lab 1.1 Defining Common Wireless Terms

Objectives

The objective of this lab is to help you learn the terminology and definitions associated with the latest wireless technologies. In this lab, you will match the correct wireless term with a definition.

After completing this lab, you will be able to:

➤ Understand characteristics of wireless technologies

➤ Relate wireless terms to their associated technology

Materials Required

This lab requires the following:

➤ Internet access

➤ Pencil or pen

Estimated completion time: **30 minutes**

LAB ACTIVITY

Activity

Match each term in the following bulleted list with a definition in the numbered list. Each bulleted term is used only once. Use the Internet and Web sites such as *www.whatis.com* and *www.webopedia.com* if you need to search for a definition.

➤ WWAN	➤ WLAN	➤ WPAN
➤ Wi-Fi	➤ WiMAX	➤ FSO
➤ Antenna	➤ War driving	➤ Wireless adapter
➤ Hot spot	➤ WAP	➤ GSM
➤ RFID	➤ Piconet	➤ Access point
➤ Microbrowser	➤ Bluetooth	➤ WML

1. Wireless network that provides Internet connection and virtual private network access from a given location. _____

2. Telecommunications industry specification that describes how mobile phones, computers, and personal digital assistants (PDAs) can be networked easily using a short-range (about 30 feet) connection. _____

3. The act of locating and possibly exploiting connections to wireless networks while driving around. _____

4. Converts radio-frequency fields (RF) into alternating current (AC) or vice versa. _____

5. Local area network in which a user can connect through a radio connection. _____

6. Formed when at least two devices, such as a portable PC and a cellular phone, connect using Bluetooth technology. _____

7. Refers to the transmission of modulated visible or infrared (IR) beams through the atmosphere to obtain broadband communications. _____

8. Specification for a set of protocols that standardize the way wireless devices, such as cellular telephones and radio transceivers, are used for Internet access. _____

9. Incorporates the use of radio frequency to uniquely identify an object, animal, or person. _____

10. A wireless computer data network that may extend over a large geographical area. _____

11. A language that allows the text portions of Web pages to be displayed on cell phones and PDAs wirelessly. _____

12. Wireless industry coalition whose members organized to advance the IEEE 802.16 standard, which will enable wireless networks to transmit up to 30 miles. _____

13. A wireless network for interconnecting devices centered around an individual person's workspace. _____

14. Software built into a wireless device that allows users to access and display specially formatted Internet content using a handset device. _____

15. A station that transmits and receives data and connects wireless users to the wired network. _____

16. Term for certain types of wireless LANs that use specifications in the 802.11 family. _____

17. A card that is inserted into a device to connect it to a wireless network. _____

18. A WWAN technology used by cell phones and other handheld devices. _____

Certification Objectives

Objectives for the CWNA exam:

➤ Identify the technology roles for which wireless LAN technology is an appropriate technology application

Review Questions

1. What is the fundamental difference between a WLAN, WPAN, and WWAN?

2. What is the difference between a regular Web browser and a microbrowser?

3. What is the difference between HTML and WML?

4. What is the difference between Wi-Fi and WiMAX?

5. What are the advantages and disadvantages to using a hot spot?

LAB 1.2 COMPARING WIRELESS SYSTEMS TO WIRED SYSTEMS

Objectives

Although they are both types of networks, there are fundamental differences between wired networks and wireless networks. It is important to understand these differences when deciding if wireless is right for your home or business. The objective of this lab is to compare wired networks with wireless networks.

In this lab, you will decide whether a given networking feature is an advantage of wireless over wired or wired over wireless. You will defend your answer.

After completing this lab, you will be able to:

➤ Explain the advantages and disadvantages of wireless networking

Materials Required

This lab requires the following:

➤ Pen or pencil

Estimated completion time: **20 minutes**

ACTIVITY

1. The first column of Table 1-1 contains advantages of wireless over wired systems or wired over wireless systems. Match each advantage to a system by writing either "Wired" or "Wireless" in the second column. You may believe that neither wireless nor wired systems have an advantage. In the third column, defend your choice.

Table 1-1   Advantages of Wired or Wireless Systems

Advantage	Wired or Wireless	Explain
Interference		
Installation		
Security		
Mobility		
Disaster recovery		
Reliability		
Health risks		

Certification Objectives

Objectives for the CWNA exam:

This lab does not map to a certification objective; however, it contains information that will be beneficial to your professional development.

Review Questions

1. Interference is not a concern with wired networks. True or False?

2. The primary advantage of wireless systems is mobility. True or False?

3. Explain the difference between a hot site and a cold site.

4. Why are wireless networks inherently less secure than wired networks?

5. In your opinion, is wireless better than wired for regular desktop computing when mobility is not a factor? Why or why not?

LAB 1.3 EXPLORING THE DIFFERENCES BETWEEN BLUETOOTH AND WI-FI

Objectives

Bluetooth and Wi-Fi are competing wireless standards, but the mission of these two systems is somewhat different. Bluetooth is a WPAN technology and Wi-Fi is a WLAN technology. Many have wondered if Bluetooth was on its way to extinction, but lately there seems to be a resurgence of interest in Bluetooth devices. The objective of this lab is to research Bluetooth and Wi-Fi so that you understand the similarities and differences between them.

In this lab you will browse some Web sites that will give you insight into these competing standards.

After completing this lab, you will be able to:

➤ Describe the differences and similarities between Bluetooth and Wi-Fi systems

Materials Required

This lab requires the following:

➤ Internet access

Estimated completion time: **30 minutes**

LAB ACTIVITY

ACTIVITY

1. Browse to *www.bluetooth.com* using your Internet browser.

2. What are some of the latest Bluetooth devices?

   _____

3. Browse to *www.whatis.com*. Search for **802.xx**. Scroll down and click **802.xx Fast Reference**.

4. Scroll down and click the **802.15** link. How is 802.15 related to Bluetooth?

   _____

5. Click the **Back** button in your browser to return to the 802.xx Fast Reference Web page.

6. Click the **Wi-Fi** link. What is "Wi-Fi" short for? _____

7. To which IEEE standard did Wi-Fi originally apply? _____

   What IEEE standards does Wi-Fi apply to now? _____

8. Browse to *www.dell.com/downloads/global/power/di2q04-005.pdf*. Scroll down to the Bluetooth versus Wi-Fi table. What are Bluetooth devices designed to do?

   _____

   What are Wi-Fi devices designed to do?

   _____

9. What is the range of Bluetooth devices versus the range of Wi-Fi devices?

   _____

10. Bluetooth devices interfere with some Wi-Fi devices. Why is this true?

    _____

11. Close your browser.

Certification Objectives

Objectives for the CWNA exam:

➤ Identify, apply, and comprehend the differences between wireless LAN standards

➤ Understand the roles of organizations in providing direction and accountability with the wireless LAN industry

Review Questions

1. What is the IEEE standard for Bluetooth?

2. What is the IEEE standard for Wi-Fi?

3. In what way are Bluetooth and Wi-Fi competing standards?

4. In what way are Bluetooth and Wi-Fi *not* competing standards?

5. How do you feel about the prospects of Bluetooth? Why?

WIRELESS LAN DEVICES AND STANDARDS

Labs included in this chapter

➤ Lab 2.1 Installing and Configuring a Cisco Wireless Adapter on a Laptop Running Windows XP

➤ Lab 2.2 Accessing the Cisco Aironet 1200 Access Point Using HyperTerminal

➤ Lab 2.3 Configuring the Cisco Aironet 1200 Access Point Using Internet Explorer

➤ Lab 2.4 Monitoring the Wireless Connection Using Cisco's Aironet Desktop Utility

➤ Lab 2.5 Configuring the Wireless Connection Using Cisco's Aironet Desktop Utility

CWNA Exam Objectives	
Objective	**Lab**
Recognize the concepts associated with wireless LAN service sets	2.1
Identify the purpose of infrastructure devices and how to install, configure, and manage them	2.2, 2.3
Identify the purpose of LAN client devices and how to install, configure, and manage them	2.1, 2.4, 2.5

Lab 2.1 Installing and Configuring a Cisco Wireless Adapter on a Laptop Running Windows XP

Objectives

Three steps are involved in setting up a wireless client: The wireless adapter is installed, the drivers for the adapter are loaded, and then the client utilities to manage the adapter are installed. The purpose of this lab is to start a simple, peer-to-peer wireless network, which does not involve a wireless access point. Instead, wireless clients communicate directly with each other. A peer-to-peer wireless network is more commonly known as an ad hoc network.

Wireless networks have names to distinguish them from each other. A wireless network name usually is referred to as an SSID (Service Set Identifier). In this lab, you will use your team name as your network name. This will distinguish your ad hoc network from the other teams' networks.

The labs in this chapter, as well as in most of this lab manual, involve working in teams. A team is a group of two to four people sharing two laptops and one access point.

In this lab, you will set up a simple ad hoc network and communicate between your team's two laptops.

After completing this lab, you will be able to:

➤ Set up a wireless client

➤ Understand the concept of an SSID

➤ Understand the nature of an ad hoc wireless network

➤ Use Windows XP to manage your wireless connection

Materials Required

This lab requires the following for each team:

➤ Two laptop computers running Windows XP with Service Pack 2, each with an available Type II PC slot

➤ Two Cisco Aironet a/b/g adapters

➤ Cisco Aironet drivers and utilities CD (files also provided on student CD)

Estimated completion time: **30 minutes**

ACTIVITY

LAB ACTIVITY

NOTE

If you already have installed and configured a Cisco wireless adapter in a previous activity, begin with Step 3. If you also have previously installed the Cisco Aironet drivers and utilities, begin with Step 6.

2

1. You will do the following activities on both of your team's laptops. Begin by making sure the laptops are off.

2. Hold the Cisco 802.11 a/b/g adapter with the Cisco logo facing up and insert it into the laptop. Apply just enough pressure to make sure the adapter is seated. Turn on the laptop. Log on as **administrator**. If the Found New Hardware Wizard opens, click **Cancel** to close the window.

3. Insert the CD that contains the drivers and utilities. A window should open automatically and display a file named Win-Client-802.11a-b-g-Ins-Wizard-v1.exe. Double-click the file to install it. If the CD doesn't open automatically, browse for the file and then double-click it to install it.

4. Follow the directions to install the adapter drivers and utilities using the default settings and recommended selections.

5. Reboot when instructed.

6. Log on to both laptops. You now should have an Aironet Desktop Utility icon on your desktop. Click **Start**, then click **Control Panel**. The Control Panel should be using Category View. If it is in Classic View, click **Switch to Category View**. Click **Network and Internet Connections**, and then click **Network Connections**.

7. Many laptops now come with onboard wireless equipment. An additional wireless connection may interfere with the Cisco connection you just configured. If the Network and Internet Connections window indicates that your laptop has a wireless connection in addition to the Cisco connection you just configured, right-click the additional wireless connection and click **Disable**.

8. Right-click the **Wireless Network Connection** associated with your Cisco Aironet adapter. Click **Rename**. Type **Cisco Wireless Adapter** and press **Enter**. Right-click the **Cisco Wireless Adapter** and click **Properties**.

9. On the General tab, double-click **Internet Protocol (TCP/IP)** and click **Use the following IP address**. Configure the IP address and subnet mask of your laptop according to Table 2-1. There is no default gateway because you will be communicating in ad hoc mode. Click **OK** to return to the Properties window when you finish configuring the IP address.

Table 2-1   IP addresses for laptops

Laptop name	IP address	Subnet mask
Alpha	192.168.100.3	255.255.255.0
Bravo	192.168.100.4	255.255.255.0
Charlie	192.168.100.5	255.255.255.0
Delta	192.168.100.6	255.255.255.0
Echo	192.168.100.7	255.255.255.0
Foxtrot	192.168.100.8	255.255.255.0
Golf	192.168.100.9	255.255.255.0
Hotel	192.168.100.10	255.255.255.0
India	192.168.100.11	255.255.255.0
Juliet	192.168.100.12	255.255.255.0

10. Click the **Wireless Networks** tab. Check **Use Windows to configure my wireless network settings** if necessary. You also can use the Aironet Desktop Utility (ADU) to configure your connection. You will use the ADU in a later lab.

11. Under Preferred Networks, click **Add**.

12. Type a **Network Name (SSID)** based on Table 2-2. This is also your team name. Type the SSID exactly as it is shown; SSIDs are case sensitive.

Table 2-2   Network names

Laptop name	Network name (SSID)
Alpha	alpha-bravo
Bravo	alpha-bravo
Charlie	charlie-delta
Delta	charlie-delta
Echo	echo-foxtrot
Foxtrot	echo-foxtrot
Golf	golf-hotel
Hotel	golf-hotel
India	india-juliet
Juliet	india-juliet

13. If data encryption is configured for WEP, click the **Data encryption** drop-down arrow and select **Disabled** to disable WEP encryption. Check **This is a computer-to-computer (ad hoc) network: wireless access points are not used** and then click **OK**. The new network should appear in the Preferred Networks window. Click **OK** to close the Connection Properties window.

14. Once your team has both laptops configured, the Cisco Wireless Adapter icon in the Network Connections window should indicate an up status. Click the connection icon (which depicts two computers communicating) in the tray at the bottom right of your screen. What is the status of your connection?

What is the speed? _____

How good is your signal strength? _____

15. Click **Start**, then click **Run**. Type **cmd** and press **Enter** to get to the command prompt.

16. Type **ping** followed by the computer name of your partner's laptop. This should be a successful ping, indicated by a series of replies. Ask the instructor for help if it is not successful.

17. Close all windows and remove the CD if necessary.

18. Shut down both laptops.

Certification Objectives

Objectives for the CWNA exam:

➤ Recognize the concepts associated with wireless LAN service sets

➤ Identify the purpose of LAN client devices and how to install, configure, and manage them

Review Questions

1. What are the three steps involved in setting up a wireless client?

2. What is another name for an ad hoc network?

3. In ad hoc mode, wireless clients communicate with each other directly. No access point is necessary. True or False?

4. What is the network name often called when you configure wireless networks?

5. You must use Windows to monitor and configure your wireless connection if your computer is running Windows XP. True or False?

Lab 2.2 Accessing the Cisco Aironet 1200 Access Point Using HyperTerminal

Objectives

Several methods and interfaces are available for access point configuration. The Hyper-Terminal program can be one of the most confusing methods, because the interface is not user friendly. However, HyperTerminal allows you to configure the access point while physically attached to it via a console cable. This means that you do not need network access to configure it. Once you gain entry to the access point via HyperTerminal, the functionality of the interface depends on whether the firmware in the access point has been upgraded from the standard VxWorks interface to the Cisco IOS interface. The access point used in the lab should have been upgraded to the IOS.

If you are familiar with configuring Cisco routers and switches, you will probably recognize the command line interface (CLI). This interface is prompt- and syntax-specific and difficult to learn. In this lab, you will use a few basic commands to gain familiarity with the interface. You also will configure a new IP address for the bridge group virtual interface so you can access the 1200 using a Web browser in Lab 2.3. When using the CLI you can get help at any time by typing the question mark, which displays all the commands you can use from the displayed prompt.

In this lab, you will learn how to access and configure your access point using Hyper-Terminal and Cisco's command-line interface.

After completing this lab, you will be able to:

➤ Explain the purpose of the HyperTerminal program

➤ Describe the equipment necessary to connect locally to an access point for configuration via HyperTerminal

➤ Understand the HyperTerminal settings necessary to establish a successful local connection to the access point

➤ Describe the basic Cisco commands used to display the access point's configuration and interface information, and to configure an IP address

Materials Required

This lab requires the following for each team:

➤ One laptop with a serial port running Windows XP with Service Pack 2 and configured with a Cisco Aironet adapter

➤ One Cisco Aironet 1200 access point using IOS-based firmware and interface

➤ Power cable for the Cisco Aironet 1200

➤ One console (rollover) cable

➤ One DB-9-to-RJ-45 adapter (may not be necessary if console cable has one DB-9 end)

2

Estimated completion time: **30 minutes**

LAB ACTIVITY

ACTIVITY

1. Turn on one of your team's laptops and log on.

2. Refer to Figure 2–1 and attach a DB-9-to-RJ-45 adapter to the COM1 port on the back of the laptop. Connect a rollover cable to the DB-9-to-RJ-45 adapter. Attach the other end of the cable to the console port on the back of your team's access point.

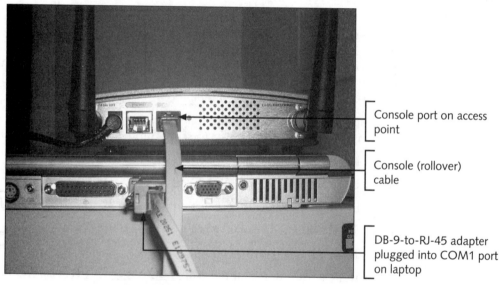

Console port on access point

Console (rollover) cable

DB-9-to-RJ-45 adapter plugged into COM1 port on laptop

Figure 2-1   Console connection

3. Turn on the access point if necessary by plugging it in.

4. Click **Start**, point to **All Programs**, point to **Accessories**, point to **Communications**, and click **HyperTerminal**. Click **Yes** if prompted to make HyperTerminal your default telnet program.

5. Click **Cancel** to cancel the dial-up information window if it appears.

6. In the Connection Description window, type the name of your connection, which should be your team name. For example, if you are team alpha–bravo, enter it as your connection name. Click **OK**.

7. When the Connect To dialog box appears, change the Connect Using entry to **COM1** and click **OK**.

8. Configure the settings in the COM1 Properties window, as shown in Table 2-3, and then click **OK**.

Table 2-3 HyperTerminal settings

Bits Per Second:	9600
Data Bits:	8
Parity:	None
Stop Bits:	1
Flow Control:	Xon/Xoff

9. Text appears in the HyperTerminal window. If text does not appear immediately, press **Enter**. Eventually, the ap> prompt displays. Thus, the default name of the access point is ap. The greater-than sign after the name indicates that you are in user mode. No configuration or damage can be done in this mode.

10. Type **enable** and press **Enter**. You are prompted for a password. Type **Cisco**, which is the default password for this particular IOS, and press **Enter**. (This password is case sensitive.) Notice that the password does not display as you type it. Notice also that the prompt changes to ap#. This is privileged mode, which also is known as enable mode.

11. Type **show run** and press **Enter**. The current configuration of the access point appears. Press the Spacebar to scroll through the output as necessary.

    What is the name of the radio interface? _Dot 11 radio 0_

    What is the default SSID? _CRWaP_

    What is the name of the Ethernet interface? ~~☒~~ _Fastethernet 0_

    Press the Spacebar as necessary until the ap# prompt displays again.

12. Type **show int dot11radio0** and press **Enter**.

    What is the MAC address of the radio? _0026.993c.0830_ ✓

    What is the BIA (burned-in address) of the radio? _____ ✓

    What is the bandwidth (BW) of the radio in Mbps? _54_

    What 802.11 standard is the radio using? _802.11g_

13. Type **show int f0** and press **Enter**.

    What is the MAC address of the Ethernet interface? _0026.0B4D.5f2c_

    What is the BIA of the Ethernet interface? _0026.0B4D.5f2c_

    What is the bandwidth of the Ethernet interface in Mbps? _100_

14. Type **show int bvi1** and press **Enter**. What is the MAC address of the BVI?
 ~~0026.99xc.a~~ 0026. 0b4b, 5f2c

What is the BIA of the BVI? _0026. 99C. 0830_

What is the bandwidth (BW) of the BVI in Mbps? _54_

What is the default IP address of the BVI? _192. 168.202_

15. Your instructor should assign IP address information for the classroom access points. Get the IP information from your instructor and write it in the appropriate cell in Table 2-4. Use the following commands and the correct IP information to configure a new IP for the BVI interface:

conf t [Enter]

int bvi1 [Enter]

ip address [substitute the correct IP address] [substitute the correct subnet mask] **[Enter]**

no shutdown [Enter]

exit [Enter]

ip default-gateway [substitute the default gateway]

Table 2-4   Instructor-assigned IP configuration information for access points

Team name	Assigned IP address for access point	Subnet mask	Default gateway
Alpha-Bravo			
Charlie-Delta			
Echo-Foxtrot	192.168.100.2	255.255.255.0	192.168.100.1
Golf-Hotel			
India-Juliet			
Kilo-Lima (instructor laptops)			

16. Press **Ctrl+Z**. Press **Enter** to clear the message that appears.

17. Type **copy run start** and press **Enter**. Press **Enter** again when prompted. Your new IP configuration is saved on your access point.

18. Close all windows but save your connection when prompted. Shut down the laptop.

19. Remove the console cable from the laptop and the access point.

Certification Objectives

Objectives for the CWNA exam:

➤   Identify the purpose of infrastructure devices and how to install, configure, and manage them

Review Questions

1. What Windows program allows you to configure an access point directly through the console port?   *Hyper terminal, Putty*

2. No device configuration can be done when operating in Cisco's user mode. *True* or False?

3. Is the MAC address always the same as the burned-in address (BIA)?   *No*

4. What Cisco command will display the running configuration on the access point?   *Sh run*

5. What Cisco command is used to configure an IP address on an access point?   *ip address*

Lab 2.3 Configuring the Cisco Aironet 1200 Access Point Using Internet Explorer

Objectives

Several methods and interfaces are available for access point configuration. In Lab 2.2, you used HyperTerminal to configure the access point directly via its console port. In this lab, you will use Internet Explorer to configure the access point. Using a Web browser such as Internet Explorer is one of the easiest ways to configure a device, but it is less safe and more limited than using a direct connection via the console port and HyperTerminal. Using a Web browser to configure your access point requires that you have network access to the device. This in turn requires that your access point has been configured with an IP address that is reachable from your laptop.

In this lab, you will configure your access point using Internet Explorer.

After completing this lab, you will be able to:

➤ Connect to your access point via Internet Explorer

➤ Navigate through Cisco's browser interface

➤ Configure the Cisco Aironet 1200 access point using a Web browser

Materials Required

This lab requires the following for each team:

➤ Two laptop computers running Windows XP with Service Pack 2 and configured with a Cisco Aironet adapter

➤ One Cisco Aironet 1200 access point using IOS-based firmware and interface

➤ Power cable for the Cisco Aironet 1200

➤ One Ethernet switch for the classroom connected to the Internet through the facility's network infrastructure (only one switch is required, regardless of the number of teams)

➤ One UTP patch cable

➤ Power cable for the switch

Estimated completion time: **30 minutes**

ACTIVITY

1. Connect your access point to a switch port using a regular UTP patch cable. The patch cable should connect to the Ethernet port on the access point. The lab setup is shown in Figure 2-2. Power up the access point if necessary. Turn on the laptops and log on.

2. On both of your team's laptops, click **Start**, click **Control Panel**, point to **Network and Internet Connections**, and click **Network Connections**.

3. Right-click the **Cisco Wireless Adapter** and click **Properties**.

4. Double-click **Internet Protocol (TCP/IP)** and click **Obtain an IP address automatically**. Click **OK**.

5. Point to the ADU icon in the tray. If you are connected to tsunami, skip to Step 8.

6. Click the **Wireless Networks** tab and then click the **Advanced** button. Select **Any available network (access point preferred)** if necessary. Click **Close**. Click **tsunami** in the Available Networks window if it is displayed. Click the **Configure** button. Click **OK** twice.

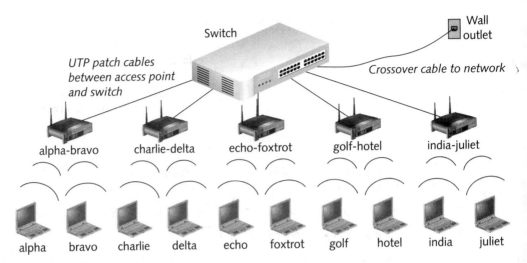

Figure 2-2   Basic lab setup

7. If the tsunami connection is up, go to Step 8. If the connection is not up, double-click the **Wireless Connection** icon in the Network Connections window and make sure that **tsunami** is selected. Click **Allow me to connect, even if not secure**. Click **Connect**. At this point, the connection should be up. Ask your instructor for help if you have problems connecting.

8. Click **Start**, then click **Internet Explorer**. The program should detect proxy settings and connect to the Internet.

9. In the URL text box, enter the IP address of the access point that you configured in Step 15 of Lab 2.2. You may need to type **http://** in front of the actual IP address. Press **Enter**. When prompted for a username and password, enter **administrator** as the username and **Cisco** as the password. (The password is case sensitive.) Click **OK** to gain access to the access point.

10. Click **Home** if necessary. How many clients are connected to your access point? __3__

    What is the speed of the Fast Ethernet connection? _100 mBPS_
    What is the speed of the radio connection? _54 MBPS_

11. Click **Association**. What are the names, IP addresses, and MAC addresses of the connected clients?

    HNRMCG1 - 10.17.178.33 - 0040.96b5.bf89
    None - 10.230.99.174 - 7cf.938.81sc
    None - 10.17.178.34 - c600.c2/32.8091

12. Click **Network Interfaces**. What is the status of the Fast Ethernet interface? <u>Enabled</u>

    What is the status of the Radio interface? <u>Enabled</u>

    They should both be enabled and up.

2

13. Click **Radio0-802.11G**. (Note that your interface may indicate A or B rather than G.) What is your current radio channel? <u>4</u>

14. Click **Express Set-Up**. What is the name of the access point? <u>Team CR</u>

15. Click **System Software**. What is the system software filename? <u>c1240-k9w7-tar 124-3la, JA1</u>

16. Click **Software Upgrade**. What two protocols can you use to upgrade your firmware? <u>tftp, http</u>

17. Click **Express Security** or just **Security** if you do not have the Express Security option. What is the SSID? <u>Team CRWAP</u>

    Is the SSID being broadcast by the access point? <u>yes</u>

    What type of security is being used? <u>None</u>   <u>wep, radius, wPA</u>

    What are some security options on the Cisco 1200? <u>Encryption, Authen</u>

18. On only one of the laptops, click **Security**, then click **SSID Manager**. Enter a new SSID in the SSID text box, which should be your team name with "wap" added to the end (for example, charlie-deltawap). Scroll down to the first instance of **Apply** and click it. Click **OK** to save the new SSID.

19. When the SSID Manager window appears again, scroll to the bottom of the window and set **Guest Mode** for your new SSID. If your new SSID doesn't appear, click **Home**, click **Security**, and then click **SSID Manager** again to refresh the screen. Guest Mode means that your access point will broadcast this new SSID. Click the bottom instance of **Apply** and then click **OK** to save the setting. Minimize the window.

20. On both laptops, right-click your wireless connection in the tray and click **Open Network Connections**.

21. Right-click the **Cisco Wireless Adapter** icon and click **Properties**.

22. Click the **Wireless Networks** tab. Make sure that **Use Windows to configure my wireless network settings** is selected. Look for the new network SSID in the Available Networks window. You may need to click the **View Wireless Networks** button, then click **Refresh Network List** to

make it appear. If tsunami is in the list, click it and then click **Disconnect**. In a few seconds, you should connect to the access point using the new SSID. If you do not connect, try rebooting your laptop. Point to the ADU icon in the tray; this icon is green if you are connected. Are you associated with the new SSID? _Yes_

Ask your instructor for help if you have problems associating with your access point.

23. Maximize Internet Explorer. Click **Home** and scroll to the bottom of the display. The event log should indicate that your radio interface went down but then came back up. How did the laptop know about the new SSID? _Radio Assication_

24. Click **Security**. The new SSID should appear in the Radio section of the table.

25. Close the Web browser and return to the Network Connections window. Right-click **Cisco Wireless Adapter** and click **Properties**.

26. Click the **Wireless Networks** tab. You should see two or three different SSIDs listed. What does each represent? _echo - foxtrot, team CAWAP_

27. Close all windows. Shut down your laptop.

Certification Objectives

Objectives for the CWNA exam:

➤   Identify the purpose of infrastructure devices and how to install, configure, and manage them

Review Questions

1. Unlike a direct connection via the console port, using a Web browser to configure an access point requires a network connection and valid configured IP addresses. (True) or False?

2. What is the function of the SSID? _Network Identification_

3. Why might you want to configure multiple SSIDs?

    Multiple Networks

4. By default, you cannot connect to an access point without knowing the SSID. (True) or False?

5. Why might you want to disable Web browser access on your access point and only use the console port for configuration purposes?

    Security

LAB 2.4 MONITORING THE WIRELESS CONNECTION USING CISCO'S AIRONET DESKTOP UTILITY

Objectives

When you installed the Cisco wireless adapter in Lab 2.1, the accompanying software included a program called the Aironet Desktop Utility (ADU). The ADU can be used to configure your laptop's wireless connection via profiles. In previous labs, you used Microsoft Windows to configure your wireless connections. In this lab and for the remainder of this manual, you will use the ADU. You will find using Cisco's own client utilities much more intuitive than using Windows' generic wireless configuration tools. In addition to configuration, the ADU provides link status, statistics, IP configuration, frequency, bandwidth, and channel information, and a means of troubleshooting your connection. The purpose of this lab is to expose you to some of the features of the ADU.

In this lab, you will use Cisco's Aironet Desktop Utility to examine your wireless connection.

After completing this lab, you will be able to:

➤ Understand the features of Cisco's Aironet Desktop Utility

Materials Required

This lab requires the following for each team:

➤ Two laptop computers running Windows XP with Service Pack 2 and configured with a Cisco Aironet adapter

➤ One Cisco Aironet 1200 access point using IOS-based firmware and interface

➤ Power cable for the Cisco Aironet 1200

➤ One Ethernet switch for the classroom connected to the Internet through the facility's network infrastructure (only one switch is required, regardless of the number of teams)

➤ One UTP patch cable

➤ Power cable for the switch

Estimated completion time: **15 minutes**

LAB ACTIVITY

ACTIVITY

1. Turn on the laptops and log on. Connect your team's access point to the switch if necessary. Plug in your access point if necessary.

2. Double-click the ADU shortcut on your desktop to open this utility. What is your profile name? _Echo-foxhot_

   What is your link status? _Associated_

   What is your server-based authentication? _None_

   Are you using data encryption? _None_

   What network type are you participating in? _Infrastructure_

   What channel are you using? _4_

   What is your frequency and bandwidth? _2.4GHz   54mbps_

   What is your IP address? _10.17.118.3?_

   What is your signal strength? _excellent._

3. Click the **Profile Management** tab. This allows you to add to and modify your profiles.

4. Click the **Diagnostics** tab. This gives you information regarding your wireless adapter, as well as transmit and receive statistics.

5. Click the **Troubleshooting** button. Click the **Run Test** button. The utility tests various parameters related to your adapter's installation, configuration, and operation.

6. Click the **View Report** button. Scroll down to investigate the results of the diagnostic tests. What type of NIC do you have? _Cisco   Aironet   802.11 AP_

   Why was the authentication test bypassed? _None_

   What is your access point's IP address? _10.17.178.40_

   Was your laptop able to ping the access point successfully? _Yes_

7. Close the ADU windows.

8. Point to the **ADU** icon in the tray at the bottom of your screen to see a pop-up menu. What valuable information is available just by pointing to this icon?

   Profile, SSid, Association, Strengh, Speed, IP
   Address,

9. Shut down your laptops.

Certification Objectives

Objectives for the CWNA exam:

➤ Identify the purpose of LAN client devices and how to install, configure, and manage them

Review Questions

1. Why is using Cisco's client utility (ADU) to monitor the client better than using Windows? _more options, test ability, more information,_

2. What are some of the features included with the ADU?
   Testing, Security

3. What is the Cisco default for encryption?
   None

4. What is the Cisco default for authentication?
   None

5. Client utilities are useful for troubleshooting a connection. True or False?
   True

Lab 2.5 Configuring the Wireless Connection Using Cisco's Aironet Desktop Utility

Objectives

In Lab 2.4 you became familiar with the ADU. You saw that there is a default profile configured for your wireless adapter. A profile defines the client connection. Often it is helpful to have multiple profiles configured so that you can connect easily to different wireless networks depending on where you are. For example, you may want an unsecured connection configured to connect to public hot spots. At home, you may use a different profile to connect to your personal wireless device using some basic security settings. The purpose of this lab is to use the ADU to make changes to your wireless adapter's configuration by creating additional profiles, then examining the effect the new profiles have with respect to your wireless network. You will create a 5-GHz infrastructure mode profile, a 2.4-GHz infrastructure mode profile, and a 2.4-GHz ad hoc mode profile.

In this lab, you will use Cisco's Aironet Desktop Utility to configure multiple client profiles.

After completing this lab, you will be able to:

➤ Understand the purpose of profiles

➤ Understand how to configure profiles

➤ Understand the difference between infrastructure mode and ad hoc mode

Materials Required

This lab requires the following for each team:

➤ Two laptop computers running Windows XP with Service Pack 2 and configured with a Cisco Aironet adapter

➤ One Cisco Aironet 1200 access point using IOS-based firmware and interface

➤ Power cable for the Cisco Aironet 1200

➤ One Ethernet switch for the classroom connected to the Internet through the facility's network infrastructure (only one switch is required, regardless of the number of teams)

➤ One UTP patch cable

➤ Power cable for the switch

Estimated completion time: **15 minutes**

LAB ACTIVITY

ACTIVITY

1. Connect and power up your team's access point if necessary. Turn on both of your laptops and log on. You will perform the following steps on both laptops.

2. Right-click your wireless connection in the tray and click **Open Network Connections**.

3. Right-click **Cisco Wireless Adapter** and click **Properties**.

4. Click the **Wireless Networks** tab and deselect **Use Windows to configure my wireless network settings**. Click **OK** and then close the Network Connections window.

5. Double-click the ADU shortcut on your desktop to open this utility.

6. Click the **Profile Management** tab.

7. Click the **New** button to add a new profile with the following parameters:

   Profile Name: **Airport**

   Client Name: Use your computer name, which already should be displayed.

8. Click the **Security** tab and make sure that **None** is selected.

9. Click the **Advanced** tab. You now will intentionally deselect the radio frequency used by your access point. If your access point is using an 802.11a radio, deselect the 5-GHz option. If your access point is using an 802.11b or g radio, deselect the 2.4-GHz options. Leave infrastructure mode as the network type.

10. Click **OK** to create the Airport profile.

11. Switch to the Airport profile by double-clicking the name **Airport**. Did you lose your connection? ___*NO*___

    If you did, why do you think this is so?

    _____

12. Click **New** to create another new profile with the following parameters:

    Profile Name: **Infrastructure Mode**

    Client Name: Use your computer name, which already should be displayed.

    SSID1: Use your team name with "wap" appended—for example, india-julietwap. This is the same SSID you configured in Lab 2.3.

13. Click the **Security** tab and make sure that **None** is selected.

14. Click the **Advanced** tab. Make sure that **Infrastructure** is the network type and that all wireless modes are selected.

15. Click the **Preferred AP's** button and enter the MAC address of your access point's radio as recorded in Step 12 of Lab 2.2. (Don't use any periods or dashes.) Click **OK**.

16. Click **OK** again to create the Infrastructure Mode profile.

17. Double-click the **Infrastructure Mode** profile to activate it. If you don't connect, click **Scan** and then click **Refresh**. Eventually you should connect.

18. Click **New** to create another new profile with the following parameters:

    Profile Name: **Ad Hoc Mode**

    Client Name: Use your computer name, which already should be displayed.

    SSID1: Use your team name—for example, golf-hotel. This is the same SSID you configured in Lab 2.1 when you set up an ad hoc network.

19. Click the **Security** tab and make sure that **None** is selected.

20. Click the **Advanced** tab. Change Infrastructure to **Ad hoc** for the network type.
21. Click **OK** to create the Ad Hoc Mode profile.
22. Close the ADU window with Infrastructure Mode still activated.
23. Shut down your laptops.

Certification Objectives

Objectives for the CWNA exam:

➤ Identify the purpose of LAN client devices and how to install, configure, and manage them

Review Questions

1. What is the purpose of profiles?

   To Allow Connection to Different Networks

2. Explain the difference between infrastructure mode and ad hoc mode.

   infrastructure has AP, Ad hoc is Peer to Peer.

3. What is the point of configuring the MAC address of your access point in a profile?

   for Identification

4. What is the point of configuring an SSID in a profile?

   connection to right Network

5. List three different profiles you would find useful.

   Airport

How Wireless Works

Labs included in this chapter

➤ Lab 3.1 Performing RF Math Calculations

➤ Lab 3.2 Calculating the Fresnel Zone Radius

➤ Lab 3.3 Investigating Cisco Aironet Antenna Specifications

➤ Lab 3.4 Investigating the Relationship Between Range and Signal Strength Using a Linksys Wireless Router

CWNA Exam Objectives	
Objective	Lab
Understand and apply the basic components of RF mathematics	3.1
Understand the applications of basic RF antenna concepts	3.2
Explain the concepts of polarization, gain, beamwidth, and free-space path loss as these concepts apply to implementing solutions that require antennas	3.3
Identify the basic attributes, purpose, and function of antenna types	3.3
Identify and apply the concepts that make up the functionality of spread spectrum technology	3.4
Recognize concepts associated with wireless LAN service sets	3.4

Lab 3.1 Performing RF Math Calculations

Objectives

One of the duties of a wireless network administrator is to manage power emitted from wireless devices on the network and to make sure the signal is being received at the destination. Because power is regulated by the FCC, even in unlicensed bands like the ones used in 802.11 networks, you must master the calculation of power levels. The total power of the signal from your antenna is referred to as Equivalent (or Effective) Isotropic Radiated Power, or EIRP. EIRP is typically measured in dBi, which is relative, instead of dBm, which is an absolute measure of power. You can perform RF power calculations using power formulas or by estimating using the rule of 10's and 3's.

In this lab, you will sharpen your RF math skills by performing power calculations using both power formulas and the rule of 10's and 3's.

After completing this lab, you will be able to:

➤ Use power calculations to convert from dBm to milliwatts

➤ Use power calculations to convert from milliwatts to dBm

➤ Use power calculations to calculate change in power

➤ Estimate power using the rule of 10's and 3's

Materials Required

This lab requires the following:

➤ Pencil or pen

➤ One laptop computer running Windows XP with Service Pack 2

Estimated completion time: **20 minutes**

Activity

1. Turn on your team's laptops. On each, click **Start**, point to **All Programs**, point to **Accessories**, and then click **Calculator**. If necessary, click **View** on the menu bar, then click **Scientific** to open the scientific calculator.

2. Performing RF calculations often involves converting between milliwatts and dBm. Review the following power calculation formulas.

$$P_{(dBm)} = 10 \log P_{(mW)}$$

$$P_{(mW)} = \log^{-1}(P_{(dBm)}/10)$$

$$\text{Change in Power}_{(dBm)} = 10 \log(P_{(final\ mW)}/P_{(initial\ mW)})$$

3

3. Use the correct formula to calculate what 15 watts is in dBm.

   _____

4. Use the correct formula to calculate what 31 dBm is in watts.

   _____

5. You upgrade your antenna and the EIRP increases from 50 mW to 75 mW. Calculate the change in power in dBm.

   _____

6. You can estimate power without the formulas using the rule of 10's and 3's. The relationship between dBm and mW is shown in Table 3-1. Notice that as mW increases by factors of 10, dBm increases by adding 10. Also, as mW values double, dBm increases by adding 3.

Table 3-1   Rule of 10's and 3's

10's		3's
1 mW = 0 dBm		1 mW = 0 dBm
10 mW = 10 dBm		2 mW = 3 dBm
100 mW = 20 dBm		4 mW = 6 dBm
1000 mW = 30 dBm		8 mW = 9 dBm
10,000 mW = 40 dBm		16 mW = 12 dBm
100,000 mW = 50 dBm		32 mW = 15 dBm

7. Power levels given in mW cannot be added together, but if power levels are given in dBm or dBi, you simply can add and subtract gain to get total power. What is the EIRP in dBm using a radio with a transmit power of 17 dBm, losses of 2 dBm in cables and connectors, and using a 9-dBi antenna?

   _____

   Often a power calculation problem presents itself with mixed variables. The radio transmitter power is given in mW but the gains and losses in the system are given in dBm. For example, a 16-mW transmitter with a net gain of 6 dBm could be written as:

   16 mW + 6 dBm

   The temptation is to add 6 dBm to 16 mW and get 22 mW, but that would be incorrect. The 16 mW first should be converted to dBm, then added to the 6 dBm. If you want, you then can convert the total dBm to mW.

8. Using the rule of 10's and 3's, what is 16 mW + 6 dBm in dBm? Refer to Table 3-1 for help if necessary. _____

9. Using the rule of 10's and 3's, what is 16 mW + 6 dBm in mW? Refer to Table 3-1 for help if necessary. Remember, you cannot add mW together.

   _____

10. Convert 64 mW to dBm using the correct mathematical formula shown in Step 2. _____

   Compare your answer to the answer given in Step 8. How accurate was your estimation using the rule of 10's and 3's? _____

11. Close all open windows and shut down the laptops.

Certification Objectives

Objectives for the CWNA exam:

➤ Understand and apply the basic components of RF mathematics

Review Questions

1. Why must wireless administrators learn about power calculations?

2. As milliwatts increase by a factor of 10, how does dBm increase?

3. As milliwatts increase by a factor of 2, how does dBm increase?

4. The relationship between milliwatts and dBm is linear. True or False?

5. If power units are all given in dBm, you simply can add or subtract to get the total power output. True or False?

LAB 3.2 CALCULATING THE FRESNEL ZONE RADIUS

Objectives

Power levels have much to do with successful communications. Also important is the transmission environment. In outdoor environments, blockage of the Fresnel zone is an especially important factor, although 20% to 40% blockage can be acceptable. The Fresnel zone is an oval-shaped zone around the main lobe of an RF signal. This zone must be 60% clear of trees and other obstacles to ensure good reception between outdoor wireless links. The Fresnel zone radius is widest at the center point between the two links. In Lab 3.1, you used power formulas as well as estimation techniques to calculate power. In addition to these calculations, the radius of the Fresnel zone must be known when outdoor links may experience loss of power due to Fresnel zone blockage. Fresnel zone calculations are not done in indoor environments because the distance between antennas is typically not large enough to affect communications. In addition, there are usually other impediments to transmission in indoor environments, such as concrete walls. Typical solutions to Fresnel zone blockage problems include removing the obstruction and/or raising the antennas.

3

In this lab, you learn how to calculate the radius of the Fresnel zone.

After completing this lab, you will be able to:

➤ Understand the purpose of calculating the Fresnel zone

➤ Understand how to calculate the radius of the Fresnel zone

Materials Required

This lab requires the following:

➤ Pen or pencil

➤ One laptop computer running Windows XP with Service Pack 2

Estimated completion time: **20 minutes**

ACTIVITY

1. Turn on your team's laptops. On each, click **Start**, point to **All Programs**, point to **Accessories**, and then click **Calculator**. If necessary, click **View** on the menu bar, then click **Standard** to open the standard calculator.

2. You can calculate Fresnel zone radius (in feet) by knowing the distance in miles (d) between the antennas and the frequency in GHz (f). The formula takes into consideration the allowable 40% obstruction limit. The formula to calculate the radius of the Fresnel zone at the widest point is:

$$r = 43.3 * \sqrt{\frac{d}{4f}}$$

Examine Figure 3-1. Use the Windows standard calculator to calculate the radius of the Fresnel zone.

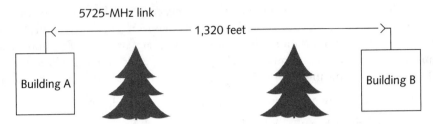

Figure 3-1 Point-to-point link

3. Figure 3-2 shows the amount of Fresnel zone blockage, which is due to trees, as shown in Figure 3-1. Do you consider this level of blockage a problem?

_____

Why or why not?

_____

If you consider this blockage a problem, what is the most obvious way to solve the problem?

_____

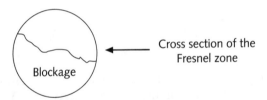

Figure 3-2 Fresnel zone blockage

4. It turns out that the trees shown in Figure 3-1 are redwoods, and an environmental group has threatened "serious consequences" if you touch a single leaf on one of the trees. What is another possible way to reduce the blockage in the Fresnel zone?

_____

5. You decide to raise the antennas to reduce Fresnel zone blockage. What effect will raising the antennas have on the radius of the Fresnel zone?

_____

6. Close all open windows and shut down the laptops.

Certification Objectives

Objectives for the CWNA exam:

➤ Understand the applications of basic RF antenna concepts

Review Questions

1. As distance between the antennas increases, what happens to the radius of the Fresnel zone?

2. As link frequency increases, what happens to the radius of the Fresnel zone?

3. What are two common solutions to a Fresnel zone blockage problem?

4. What is the maximum percentage of Fresnel zone blockage that usually can be tolerated?

5. Why aren't Fresnel zone calculations done on indoor links?

LAB 3.3 INVESTIGATING CISCO AIRONET ANTENNA SPECIFICATIONS

Objectives

The amount of online documentation available for Cisco equipment can be overwhelming. The purpose of this lab is to point you to a single location for the most pertinent information regarding the various Cisco Aironet antennas. You will investigate and record the important parameters associated with the antenna being used with your Cisco 1200 Series access point. Most likely, you are using what often are called "rubber duck" antennas. These are 4.5-inch omnidirectional (dipole) antennas that attach directly to your access point. In this lab, you will record gain, appropriate usage, horizontal and vertical beamwidths, and range for your antenna. You also will compare your antenna to an omnidirectional antenna designed specially to be mounted on the ceiling. When working with antennas, it is helpful to remember that there is a relationship between frequency and range; in general, the higher the frequency, the lower the range. In addition, there is a 6-dB rule that states for every 6 dB of gain, there is a doubling of range. You will see that there is also a relationship between bandwidth and range.

In this lab, you determine important parameters associated with your antenna.

After completing this lab, you will be able to:

➤ Locate and document Cisco Aironet antenna specifications

Materials Required

This lab requires the following:

➤ Internet access

➤ One laptop computer running Windows XP with Service Pack 2, and configured with a Cisco Aironet adapter

Estimated completion time:	15 minutes

ACTIVITY

If you are using an Internet-access computer other than the team laptops, skip to Step 3.

1. Turn on the laptops and log in. Connect your team's access point to the switch and power on if necessary.

2. Point to the **ADU** icon in the tray. You should be connected to your access point using your Infrastructure Mode profile that you created in Lab 2.5. The SSID should be your team name with the word "wap" appended to it (for example, echo-foxtrotwap). Ask your instructor for help if you have problems.

3. Open Internet Explorer and browse to **www.cisco.com**. In the next steps you will locate information regarding antenna specifications. It is possible that Web site updates have affected these steps. If you have difficulty finding the antenna specifications, search the Cisco Web site for Cisco Aironet Antennas.

4. Point to **Products and Solutions**, point to **Wireless**, and then click **All Wireless Products**.

5. Scroll down the page, if necessary, and click **Cisco Aironet Antennas and Accessories**.

6. Scroll down, if necessary, and click **Data Sheets**.

7. Click **Cisco Aironet 2.4 GHz and 5 GHz Antennas and Accessories**. Scroll down and locate your antenna type in the table. If you are using "rubber duck" antennas, your feature number may be AIR-ANT4941. What is the gain in dBi for the antenna you are using with your access point?

_____

Can the antenna you are using work outdoors as well as indoors?

_____

What is the horizontal beamwidth for your antenna? _____

What is the vertical beamwidth for your antenna? _____

What is the indoor range in feet for your antenna at 6 Mbps?

_____

What is the indoor range in feet for your antenna at 54 Mbps?

_____

8. Locate the AIR-ANT1728, which is an omnidirectional ceiling mount antenna. How does the gain on this ceiling mount antenna compare to the gain on your antenna?_____

_____

How does the range of the ceiling mount antenna compare to the range of your antenna?_____

_____

How does the vertical beamwidth of the ceiling mount antenna compare to the vertical beamwidth of your antenna?_____

_____

9. Close all windows. Shut down your laptops.

Certification Objectives

Objectives for the CWNA exam:

➤ Identify the basic attributes, purpose, and function of antenna types

➤ Explain the concepts of polarization, gain, beamwidth, and free-space path loss as these concepts apply to implementing solutions that require antennas

Review Questions

1. Why is it important to know the horizontal and vertical beamwidth of a particular antenna?

2. What is the relationship between range and frequency?

3. What is the relationship between gain and range?

4. Why do you think the horizontal beamwidth on the wall mount antennas is less than on the omnidirectional antennas?

5. What is the relationship between bandwidth and range?

LAB 3.4 INVESTIGATING THE RELATIONSHIP BETWEEN RANGE AND SIGNAL STRENGTH USING A LINKSYS WIRELESS ROUTER

Objectives

Many home users have purchased a Linksys wireless router. Linksys is now owned by Cisco and works very well with Cisco PC adapters such as the one installed in your laptop. The purpose of this lab is to investigate the setup and operation of one of these popular home routers and use it to observe the relationship between distance and signal strength. This lab includes the setup and installation of the Linksys wireless router, but that section can be skipped if you already have a Linksys wireless router configured and installed.

In this lab, you will set up a simple infrastructure network between your laptop and a Linksys wireless router. You will configure a new host name and SSID for the router. You also will observe the relationship between laptop distance from the router and signal strength.

After completing this lab, you will be able to:

➤ Set up a Linksys wireless router

➤ Understand the concept of an SSID

➤ Understand the nature of an infrastructure wireless network

➤ Use the Cisco Aironet Desktop Utility to manage your wireless connection

➤ Describe the relationship between range and signal strength on wireless connections

Materials Required

This lab requires the following:

➤ One laptop computer running Windows XP with Service Pack 2, and configured with a Cisco Aironet adapter

➤ One Linksys wireless "G" router

➤ Linksys setup wizard CD

➤ Two UTP patch cables

➤ Power cable for router

Estimated completion time: **30 minutes**

ACTIVITY

 If you already have installed and configured a Linksys wireless "G" router, begin with Step 14.

NOTE

1. You will do the following activities on one of your team's laptops. Begin by making sure the laptop is off. The router should be disconnected and powered off.

2. Using a UTP patch cable, connect your laptop's Ethernet NIC to the switch that is connected to the Internet. Turn on your laptop and log in. Make sure you have Internet connectivity before continuing.

3. Click **Start**, click **Run**, type **cmd**, and press **Enter**. Enter the **ipconfig** command. What is the IP address of your Ethernet connection?

   _____

   Close the window.

4. Insert the Linksys setup wizard CD. A window should open automatically and display the setup wizard. If the setup wizard doesn't open automatically, browse for the setup file and then double-click it to install it. Click **Click Here to Start** or click **Setup**.

5. Proceed through the wizard, following the instructions. If prompted for the static IP address settings, accept the default settings. If no default settings are displayed, configure the same settings you used for the Cisco 1200 series access point, as shown in Table 2-4 in Lab 2.2. If you did not do that lab, get new IP address settings from your instructor, if necessary.

6. Leave the domain name blank. Configure the password as **password**.

7. The wireless settings window should display. By default the router should be configured for mixed wireless mode. What is the default SSID on this router?

   _____

   What is the default channel configured on this router? _____

8. Continue through the wizard until you see the security settings. Is security mandatory on the Linksys router? _____

   What is the default security setting? _____

   Leave the default settings and continue through the wizard.

9. When prompted, confirm settings and wait as the settings are saved. Ignore any prompt to install additional software such as Symantec. Click **Finish** or **Exit** to exit the wizard.

10. With the laptop still physically connected to the Linksys router, click **Start** and then click **Run**. Type **cmd** and press **Enter**.

11. Enter the **ipconfig** command. What is the IP address of the wired NIC now?
    _____

    Is it the same as the one you recorded in Step 3? _____

    If it is different than previously recorded, why do you think this is so?

    _____

12. Close the window, then disconnect the UTP patch cable between the laptop and the router. Look at the connection icon in the tray. Are you connected wirelessly to the Linksys router? _____

    If you are connected, skip to Step 14.

13. If you are not connected wirelessly to the Linksys router, it is probably because your Cisco adapter in the laptop is using a profile, such as the Infrastructure profile created in Lab 2.5. Because this profile requires an SSID different from the one the Linksys router uses, you cannot use that profile to connect to the Linksys router without modifying the router. Double-click the **Aironet Desktop Utility** shortcut on your desktop to open the Cisco Aironet Desktop Utility. Click the **Profile Management** tab if necessary and double-click the **Default** profile to activate it. You now should be connected to the Linksys router wirelessly. Leave the window open.

14. Open Internet Explorer and browse to **192.168.1.1**. This is the default gateway of the Linksys router.

15. When prompted, enter **admin** as the username and **password** as the password. If you have previously configured a different username and password, use that login information instead. The Linksys Web browser interface should open and the basic settings should be displayed.

16. Click **Setup** if necessary. What is the default router name?
    _____

    Change the default router name to your team name (for example, alpha-bravo) Scroll down and change the time zone if necessary. Click **Save Settings** and then click **Continue**.

17. Click **Wireless**. The settings should indicate mixed mode with the SSID "linksys" on channel 6. Notice that SSID broadcasting is enabled by default. Change the SSID name to your team name followed by "wap" (for example, alpha-bravowap). Click **Save Settings** and then click **Continue**. Minimize Internet Explorer.

18. Return to the Aironet Desktop Utility program and click the **Profile Management** tab if necessary. Double-click the **Infrastructure Mode** profile to activate it, and then click the **Modify** button. If necessary, move your cursor to the SSID1 text box and enter the SSID you configured on the Linksys wireless router in Step 17. If you completed Lab 2.5, the correct SSID is already configured. Click **OK**. You should be connected to your wireless router. Point to the **ADU** icon in the tray to make sure you are connected.

19. Click the **Current Status** tab. What is your profile name?

    _____

    What is your wireless mode frequency and connection speed?

    _____

    How is your signal strength described? _____

20. Pick up your laptop and walk away from your Linksys router while watching the signal strength indicator in the Current status tab window. What is happening to the signal strength as you get farther away from the wireless router?

    _____

    Once the signal strength has degraded sufficiently, point to the **ADU** icon in the tray. What is the description of your signal strength now? _____

21. Close any open windows and remove the Linksys setup CD.

22. Shut down the laptops. If you are finished using the Linksys wireless router, disconnect it from the switch and unplug it.

Certification Objectives

Objectives for the CWNA exam:

➤ Identify and apply the concepts that make up the functionality of spread spectrum technology

➤ Recognize concepts associated with wireless LAN service sets

Review Questions

1. What is the default wireless mode setting, SSID, and channel assignment for the Linksys wireless router?

2. What does "mixed mode" indicate?

3. The Linksys wireless router can do network address translation as well as DHCP. True or False?

4. What is the default gateway for the Linksys wireless router?

5. What is the relationship between distance from the access point and wireless signal strength?

IEEE 802.11 PHYSICAL LAYER STANDARDS

Labs included in this chapter

➤ Lab 4.1 Investigating the Cisco 1200 Series Access Point Specifications

➤ Lab 4.2 Documenting the Trade-off between Range and Throughput

➤ Lab 4.3 Investigating Direct Sequence Spread Spectrum Behavior in a Co-Located Channel Environment

➤ Lab 4.4 Investigating Co-Channel Interference Using the Linksys Wireless Router

CWNA Exam Objectives	
Objective	Lab
Identify the regulations set forth by the FCC that govern spread spectrum technology, including power outputs, frequencies, bandwidths, hop times, and dwell times	4.1, 4.2
Identify, apply, and comprehend the differences between wireless LAN standards	4.1, 4.2
Identify and apply the concepts that make up the functionality of spread spectrum technology	4.1, 4.3, 4.4
Comprehend the differences between, and apply the different types of, spread spectrum technologies	4.3, 4.4
Identify, understand, correct, or compensate for wireless LAN implementation challenges	4.3, 4.4

Lab 4.1 Investigating the Cisco 1200 Series Access Point Specifications

Objectives

Reading the documentation for any new system is the best way to start learning about it. However, the amount of documentation for Cisco equipment is exhaustive, and sometimes specific information is not easy to find. The purpose of this lab is to point you to a single location for the most pertinent information regarding the Cisco 1200 Series access point and the 802.11 radios. The 802.11b standard is a Direct Sequence Spread Spectrum (DSSS) specification that supports data rates of 1, 2, 5.5, and 11 Mbps. The 802.11a standard has a maximum speed of 54 Mbps. This speed increase is due to the implementation of an advanced modulation technique known as Orthogonal Frequency Division Multiplexing (OFDM). At lower speeds, the 802.11a standard uses DSSS. The 802.11g standard also achieves a maximum speed of 54 Mbps by using OFDM, but unlike the 802.11a standard, it is backward compatible with 802.11b equipment at the lower speeds. This is because the same frequency is used by the 802.11b and 802.11g standards.

In this lab, you will record supported data rates for the 802.11a, 802.11b, and 802.11g radios, the frequency range and bandwidth, the number of nonoverlapping channels, the receive sensitivity, the range, and available power settings.

After completing this lab, you will be able to:

➤ List the data rates for the 802.11b, 802.11a, and 802.11g standards

➤ List the number of nonoverlapping channels for the 802.11b, 802.11a, and 802.11g standards

➤ List the highest transmit power options for the 802.11a and 802.11g radios

➤ List the indoor and outdoor ranges for the 802.11a and 802.11g radios

➤ Explain the concept of receive sensitivity

Materials Required

This lab requires the following:

➤ Internet access

➤ One laptop computer running Windows XP

Estimated completion time: **30 minutes**

ACTIVITY

This lab involves Internet research. The Cisco Web site that the lab depends on may have changed slightly since this lab was written. You may need to search within the Web site to find the requested information.

4

1. If you are doing this activity on your team's laptops rather than on a regular Internet computer, turn on the laptops and log in. Power up and connect your team's access point to the network switch if necessary.

2. Point to the **ADU** icon in the tray. You should be connected to your access point. If you are not connected, open the **Aironet Desktop Utility** by double-clicking its shortcut on the desktop, and click the **Profile Management** tab. If you are using the Cisco Aironet 1200 access point, double-click the **Infrastructure Mode** profile to activate it. If you are using a Linksys wireless router, double-click the **Default** profile to activate it. Ask your instructor for help if you have problems connecting to your access point.

3. Open Internet Explorer.

4. Browse to **www.cisco.com**.

5. Point to **Products and Solutions**, point to **Wireless**, and then click **Aironet 1200 Series Access Point**.

6. Scroll down the page and click **Data Sheets**.

7. Click **Cisco Aironet 1200 Series Access Point**.

8. Scroll down to the **Product Specifications** in Table 2.

9. Scroll to the **Data Rates Supported** row. What are the data rates for the 802.11g radio?

   _____

10. Scroll to the **Frequency Band and Operating Channels** row. What is the frequency range in GHz for the 802.11b and 802.11g standards in America, as measured by the FCC? _____

11. Scroll to the **Nonoverlapping Channels** row. How many nonoverlapping channels are there when using the 802.11g standard?

    _____

12. Minimize Internet Explorer and open the **Aironet Desktop Utility** using the shortcut on your desktop. Click the **Current Status** tab if necessary. How good is your signal? _____

    Click the **Advanced** button. What is your current signal strength in dBm? _____

    What is your link speed (data rate)? _____

13. Restore the Internet Explorer window, and scroll down to the **Receive Sensitivity (Typical)** row. To get the data rate recorded in Step 12, your dBm must be within the stated dBm. What is the stated dBm listed for your data rate?_____

    Are you within the receive sensitivity range? _____

14. Scroll to the **Available Transmit Power Settings** row. What is the highest transmit power option for the 802.11g radio in mW and dBm?

    _____

15. Scroll down to the **Range** row. What is the maximum distance outdoors (in feet) that your 802.11g clients can be from the access point and theoretically still experience the maximum data rate for your radio? _____

    What is the maximum distance indoors? _____

16. Click the **Back** button on your browser to return to the Data Sheets menu.

17. Click the **Cisco Aironet IEEE 802.11A 1200 Series Access Point Upgrade Kits** link.

18. Scroll down to the **Product Specifications** in Table 1.

19. What are the supported data rates for the 802.11a radio?

    _____

20. Scroll to the **Nonoverlapping Channels** row. How many nonoverlapping channels are there when using the 802.11a standard in North America?

    _____

21. Scroll to the **Available Transmit Power Settings** row. What is the highest transmit power option for the 802.11a radio in mW and dBm?

    _____

22. Scroll down to the **Range** row. What is the maximum distance outdoors (in feet) that your 802.11a clients can be from the access point and theoretically still experience the maximum data rate for your radio? _____

    What is the maximum distance indoors? _____

    Why do you think the outdoor range is greater than the indoor range?

    _____

23. Close all windows. Shut down your laptops or other Internet-access computers.

Certification Objectives

Objectives for the CWNA exam:

➤ Identify and apply the concepts that make up the functionality of spread spectrum technology

➤ Identify the regulations set forth by the FCC that govern spread spectrum technology, including power outputs, frequencies, bandwidths, hop times, and dwell times

➤ Identify, apply, and comprehend the differences between wireless LAN standards

Review Questions

1. Why isn't 802.11a compatible with 802.11b and 802.11g?

2. At what speeds is 802.11g compatible with 802.11b?

3. What technology makes it possible for the 802.11a and 802.11g standards to get speeds up to 54 Mbps?

4. You usually will have more range between the access point and the client device if you are indoors rather than outdoors. True or False?

5. Describe receive sensitivity.

Lab 4.2 Documenting the Trade-off between Range and Throughput

Objectives

Dynamic Rate Shifting (DRS), also known as Adaptive (or Automatic) Rate Selection (ARS), are terms used to describe a method of speed fallback on a wireless LAN client as distance increases from the access point. DRS attempts to match the best connection speed in response to distance as well as physical and traffic conditions so wireless connections stay reliable. Both FHSS (Frequency Hopping Spread Spectrum) and DSSS systems, and the IEEE 802.11 standard, require DRS. In general, as signal-to-noise ratios decrease, wireless clients jump to the next-lowest supported data rate. Supported data rates can be configured in three different ways on the Cisco 1200 series access point using an 802.11g radio. The

Best Range setting attempts to provide connectivity over the greatest distance from the access point but may sacrifice speed to do it. The Best Throughput setting attempts to maintain the greatest throughput over a relatively shorter distance. The Default setting provides for backward compatibility between 802.11g and 802.11b devices, which means that 802.11b data rates must be required. As a network administrator, you must understand how DRS works so you can plan for throughput, cell sizing, power outputs, and security.

In this lab, you will document the data rate boundaries for each of the three scenarios described above.

After completing this lab, you will be able to:

➤ Describe how setting the data rate on the access point to Best Range affects a wireless network

➤ Describe how setting the data rate on the access point to Best Throughput affects a wireless network

➤ Describe how setting the data rate on the access point to Default affects a wireless network

Materials Required

This lab requires the following for each team:

➤ Two laptop computers running Windows XP and configured with a Cisco Aironet adapter

➤ One Cisco Aironet 1200 access point using IOS-based firmware and interface

➤ One UTP patch cable

➤ Power cable for the access point

➤ Network access through a classroom switch

➤ Distance wheel (optional)

➤ Completion of the Chapter 2 labs

Estimated completion time: **30 minutes**

LAB ACTIVITY

ACTIVITY

1. Connect and power up your team's access point if necessary. Turn on both of your laptops and log in. You should be using the **Infrastructure Mode** profile and be associated with your access point.

2. Open Internet Explorer on one laptop. Browse to your access point using the IP address you configured in Lab 2.2 and log in with the username **administrator** and password **Cisco**.

3. Click **Network Interfaces**, click **Radio0-802.11G**, and then click the **Settings** tab. If you are using the 802.11a or 802.11b standard rather than the 802.11g standard, click the radio interface that is appropriate.

4. Scroll down to the **Data Rates** section. Click **Best Range**. What will this setting sacrifice to get the best range? _____

5. Scroll down and click **Apply**, and then click **OK**.

6. On the other laptop, double-click the shortcut to the **Aironet Desktop Utility** to open the program. Click the **Current Status** tab if necessary. Use the **Options/Display Settings** menu to change the signal-to-noise ratio units from dBm to percent. Click **OK**. Click the **Advanced** button to open the Advanced Status window.

7. Leave the Internet Explorer laptop on the desk. Take this lab manual, the laptop with the Advanced Status window open on it, and the distance wheel (optional), and stand next to your access point. Make sure the distance wheel has been reset to zero. If you do not have a distance wheel, assign one of the teammates the responsibility of stepping out the distance by estimating how many feet are in a "step."

8. Begin walking very slowly away from your access point while you roll the distance wheel (or count steps) to measure distance from the access point. You will be measuring until there is no signal. You should be watching for a drop in current link speed. Often this happens right after the statistics window indicates that your laptop is scanning. If your laptop starts scanning, stop and wait to see a drop in link speed. Record the signal-to-noise ratio (current signal strength) in percent, the new bandwidth (link speed), and your distance from the access point (range) in Table 4-1.

Table 4-1   Best Range table

Signal Strength (%)	Link Speed	Range
100	54 Mbps (or 11 Mbps)	0

9. When you run out of signal, take the laptop and the wheel back to the classroom.

10. On the Internet Explorer laptop, change the Data Rates setting in the Cisco IOS from Best Range to **Best Throughput**. What will this setting sacrifice to get the best speed?

_____

11. Click **Apply** and then click **OK**.

12. Repeat Steps 6 and 7 and record your findings in Table 4-2.

Table 4-2   Best Throughput table

Signal Strength (%)	Link Speed	Range
100	54 Mbps (or 11 Mbps)	0

13. When you run out of signal, take the laptop and the wheel back to the classroom.

14. On the Internet Explorer laptop, change the Data Rates setting in the Cisco IOS from Best Throughput to the **Default** setting by clicking the **Default** button. What compatibility issue does this setting solve?

_____

15. Repeat Steps 6 and 7 and record your findings in Table 4-3.

Table 4-3   Default settings table

Signal Strength (%)	Link Speed	Range
100	54 Mbps (or 11 Mbps)	0

16. Shut down the laptops.

Certification Objectives

Objectives for the CWNA exam:

➤ Identify the regulations set forth by the FCC that govern spread spectrum technology, including power outputs, frequencies, bandwidths, hop times, and dwell times

➤ Identify, apply, and comprehend the differences between wireless LAN standards

Review Questions

1. What data rate boundaries were you able to document using the Best Range setting?

2. The Best Range setting should have given you the best distance before the connection was lost. What are your observations regarding the Best Range setting?

3. What data rate boundaries were you able to document using the Best Throughput setting?

4. The Best Throughput setting should have given you the best throughput over the distance you walked, but may have sacrificed total distance as compared to the Best Range setting. What are your observations regarding the Best Throughput setting?

5. The Default setting is designed to make 802.11g devices compatible with 802.11b devices. In general, how did the Default setting perform, compared to the Best Range and Best Throughput settings?

LAB 4.3 INVESTIGATING DIRECT SEQUENCE SPREAD SPECTRUM BEHAVIOR IN A CO-LOCATED CHANNEL ENVIRONMENT

Objectives

Direct Sequence Spread Spectrum (DSSS) is one of the two original spread spectrum methods used by 802.11 networks. It is preferred over Frequency Hopping Spread Spectrum (FHSS) due to its lower implementation cost and faster data rates. One area in which DSSS systems are less advantageous than FHSS systems is co-location. Co-location is the placement of multiple access points in an area where their cell coverage overlaps. FHSS systems use 79 nonoverlapping channels, while DSSS systems use 11 overlapping channels. For all practical purposes, you only can co-locate three DSSS access points; otherwise, their signals will overlap and interfere with each other, thereby reducing bandwidth. Each of the three access points should be on a different channel: channel 1, channel 6, and channel 11. These channels are far enough away from each other that their frequencies barely overlap. Depending on the number of teams in your lab setup, you may be co-locating up to five access points.

In this lab, you will document DSSS behavior in a co-located, adjacent channel environment.

After completing this lab, you will be able to:

➤ Locate and change the default radio channel on the Cisco Aironet 1200 access point

➤ Find the most congested channels

Materials Required

This lab requires the following for each team:

➤ Two laptop computers running Windows XP and configured with a Cisco Aironet adapter

➤ One Cisco Aironet 1200 access point using IOS-based firmware and interface

➤ One UTP patch cable

➤ Power cable for the access point

➤ Network access through a classroom switch

➤ Completion of the Chapter 2 labs

Estimated completion time: **20 minutes**

ACTIVITY

LAB ACTIVITY

NOTE

It is important that more than one team be doing this lab in order to provide sufficient RF to be measured during the activity.

1. Connect and power up your team's access point if necessary. Turn on both of your laptops and log in. You should be using the **Infrastructure Mode** profile and be associated with your access point.

2. If you are having problems connecting your laptops to the access point, double-click the **Aironet Desktop Utility** shortcut on your desktop. Double-click **Infrastructure Mode** to activate that profile. If there are problems, click the **Scan** button and then click the **Refresh** button to scan for your network. Ask your instructor for help if you are still having problems.

3. Open Internet Explorer on one laptop. Browse to your access point using the IP address you configured in Lab 2.2 and log in with the username **administrator** and password **Cisco**.

4. Only two clients should be attached to your access point—your two laptops. If there are less than two on your network, go back to Step 3 and attempt to connect to your access point. If there are more than two clients, click **Clients** and make sure your two are listed. If another team's laptop is listed, ask them to get off your access point by switching to their Infrastructure Mode profile.

5. Click **Network Interfaces**, then click **Radio0–802.11G**. If you are using a different 802.11 specification, click the appropriate radio interface. Click the **Settings** tab.

4

6. Scroll down to the **Default Radio Channel**. How is the access point determining which channel to use?

   _____

   What channels are your laptops using? _____

   What is the center of the frequency in MHz? _____

7. Click the **Carrier Busy Test** tab. Click **Start** to start the test. Click **OK** when you get the warning window. The test will take a few seconds. You may have to try the test several times before it works as it should.

8. When the test is complete, look at the **Frequency** column. There are 11 entries. What do these entries represent?

   _____

   What are the most congested channels? _____

   What is the congestion on the most congested channel, in percent?

   _____

9. Leave the Cisco IOS browser window open on one laptop. On the other laptop, navigate to **www.wgst.com**. Click **Listen Live**, and then click **Click here to launch our stream**. If prompted to use Internet Explorer, click **Yes**. If prompted to install the latest version of Media Player, install it using the default settings. In a few seconds a streaming window will open. If the station is broadcasting commercials, you may not hear anything for a few minutes. Don't continue until you hear streaming audio.

10. On the other team laptop, start the **Carrier Busy Test** again. This will interrupt the stream for a second or two. Which channel is the busiest now?

   _____

   What is the percentage of congestion on that channel? _____

11. Leave the stream running. In the Cisco IOS browser window, click the **Settings** tab. Change the Least Congested Frequency setting to the channel indicated for your team, as shown in Table 4-4. Then click **Apply** and click **OK** to save the setting change.

Table 4-4   Channel assignment

Team Name	Channel
Alpha-Bravo	1
Charlie-Delta	2
Echo-Foxtrot	3
Golf-Hotel	4
India-Juliet	5

12. Run the **Carrier Busy Test** again. Are there any changes in the results you recorded in Step 10? _____

    If so, what changed?

    _____

13. Close all windows and shut down the laptops.

Certification Objectives

Objectives for the CWNA exam:

➤ Comprehend the differences between, and apply the different types of, spread spectrum technologies

➤ Identify and apply the concepts that make up the functionality of spread spectrum technology

➤ Identify, understand, correct, or compensate for wireless LAN implementation challenges

Review Questions

1. The Linksys wireless router defaults to channel 6. The Cisco Aironet 1200 defaults to the least congested channel. Which do you think is better and why?

2. How could you use the Carrier Busy Test feature of the Cisco Aironet 1200 for troubleshooting?

3. What are the three DSSS channels that don't overlap?

4. Why does co-location on adjacent channels degrade network performance?

5. In your opinion, would placing all the co-located devices on the same channel improve throughput or further degrade throughput? Why?

Lab 4.4 Investigating Co-Channel Interference Using the Linksys Wireless Router

4

Objectives

A common problem on wireless networks is the way co-located devices are configured. Co-locating multiple access points increases bandwidth to users and so is desirable. Very often, however, when troubleshooting wireless networks, you will find that the co-located devices have all been placed on the same channel or on adjacent channels. Devices that have overlapping cell coverage and are on adjacent channels or the same channel will interfere with each other and reduce, rather than increase, throughput to users. The problem is magnified if all of the equipment has not been supplied by the same vendor. Installers often place co-located devices on the same channel because they think this is the only way the devices can communicate on the wireless network. Intuitively, this makes sense, but the exact opposite is true. The maximum number of co-located DSSS devices is three, using channels 1, 6, and 11. Even with this configuration, there is still some channel overlap and interference, so the ideal workaround is to use only two devices on channels that do not overlap at all. Another option is to use 802.11a devices, which allows for eight nonoverlapping indoor channels. The purpose of this lab is to have multiple lab teams use different channels and then use the same channel on their co-located Linksys wireless routers. The results will be compared.

In this lab, you will use an online bandwidth meter to observe the effect of placing multiple Linksys wireless routers on different channels versus the same channel.

After completing this lab, you will be able to:

➤ Change channels on a Linksys wireless router

➤ Understand the concept of co-location

➤ Explain the difference between throughput when co-locating on different channels versus the same channel

Materials Required

This lab requires the following for each team:

➤ Two laptop computers running Windows XP and configured with a Cisco Aironet adapter

➤ One Linksys wireless "G" router

➤ One UTP patch cable

➤ Power cable for router

➤ Completion of Lab 3.4

Estimated completion time: **45 minutes**

ACTIVITY

LAB ACTIVITY

NOTE

It is important that at least one other team be doing this lab concurrently.

1. Make sure that your Cisco 1200 access point is turned off. Connect your Linksys wireless router to the network switch using the Internet port on the router and power it up. Turn on your team laptops and log in. Point to the **ADU** icon in the tray. Make sure you are connected to your own Linksys wireless router. You should be using the **Infrastructure Mode** profile with your team name and "wap" appended to it as the SSID. Ask your instructor for help if you have trouble connecting to your own wireless router.

2. On one of your laptops, open Internet Explorer and browse to **192.168.1.1**. This is the default gateway of the Linksys router.

3. When prompted, enter **admin** as the username and **password** as the password. If you have previously configured a different username and password, use that login information instead. The Linksys Web browser interface should open and the basic settings should be displayed.

4. Click **Wireless**. What is your current wireless channel? _____

5. Change your wireless channel to the channel indicated for your team in Table 4-5. Click **Save Settings**, then click **Continue**.

Table 4-5 Channel assignment

Team Name	Channel
Alpha-Bravo	1
Charlie-Delta	4
Echo-Foxtrot	7
Golf-Hotel	9
India-Juliet	11

6. On your other laptop, browse to **www.cnet.com** and search for **Bandwidth Meter** on the site. Click **Test Your Connection Speed**. The Bandwidth Meter speed test page should appear. If this page is not found, you may have to search the previous page for the correct bandwidth meter.

7. Enter the required information only. You should choose **Wireless** as your connection type. Click to begin the test, which will take a few minutes. What was your real-time speed in Mbps as determined by the bandwidth meter?

_____

8. On the laptop that is browsing your Linksys wireless router, change the channel back to channel **6**. Click **Save Settings** and then click **Continue**. Make sure that your laptops still are connected to the router and that at least one other team has its wireless router configured to use channel 6.

9. Return to the laptop with the Bandwidth Meter Web site displayed and run the test again. What was your real-time speed in Mbps as determined by the bandwidth meter?

_____

10. Close all windows and shut down the laptops.

Certification Objectives

Objectives for the CWNA exam:

➤ Comprehend the differences between, and apply the different types of, spread spectrum technologies

➤ Identify and apply the concepts that make up the functionality of spread spectrum technology

➤ Identify, understand, correct, or compensate for wireless LAN implementation challenges

Review Questions

1. Why do you think installers often put co-located wireless devices on the same channel?

2. What is the purpose of co-location?

3. What are some of the reasons your wireless users will experience far less bandwidth than they are expecting?

4. Did the co-channel bandwidth experiment report a lower speed than the first experiment, in which the wireless routers were on different channels? Is this what you expected? Why or why not?

5. Why might using 802.11a systems provide better co-location options?

5

IEEE 802.11 MEDIA ACCESS CONTROL AND NETWORK LAYER STANDARDS

Labs included in this chapter

➤ Lab 5.1 Investigating the Relationship between Signal Strength and Association

➤ Lab 5.2 Exploring Layer 2 Roaming

➤ Lab 5.3 Configuring Power Management Options Available with Cisco's 802.11 a/b/g Client Adapter

➤ Lab 5.4 Configuring Shared Key Authentication

➤ Lab 5.5 Investigating the Relationship between Fragmentation and Performance

---

CWNA Exam Objectives	
Objective	Lab
Identify and apply the processes involved in authentication and association	5.1, 5.2, 5.4
Understand the implications of power management features for wireless LANs	5.3
Specify the modes of operation involved in the movement of data traffic across wireless LANs	5.5

LAB 5.1 INVESTIGATING THE RELATIONSHIP BETWEEN SIGNAL STRENGTH AND ASSOCIATION

Objectives

When a wireless LAN client configured for Infrastructure mode powers up, it scans the frequency spectrum to see if there is an access point within its range to which it can associate. The client uses SSIDs and beacons to help it find the access points. By default the client will broadcast a request for any SSID, and all access points within range will respond. If the client is configured to connect to specific SSIDs, the request frame will contain those SSIDs only. Once a client is authenticated and associated with a particular access point, the connection quality can fluctuate. If the client is mobile and moves too far away from the access point, the quality of the link will deteriorate until the client becomes disassociated. The client will begin scanning for an access point and attempt to reassociate. Determining whether to jump to another access point is largely a function of the signal-to-noise ratio (SNR). The purpose of this lab is to configure your client to associate with your access point as well as your instructor's access point, which is on the same network, but its coverage does not overlap with your access point's coverage. This is not considered roaming. Roaming implies continuous connectivity, and cell coverage between access points must overlap at least 20% for roaming to work.

In this lab you will configure your client laptop to associate with your access point and the instructor's. You will then move the client device between the access points and observe and record the relationship between signal strength and association.

After completing this lab, you will be able to:

➤ Explain the relationship between signal strength and association

➤ Explain how a client finds an access point with which to associate

➤ Understand the role SSIDs play in the association process

Materials Required

This lab requires the following for each team:

➤ Two laptop computers running Windows XP and configured with a Cisco Aironet adapter

➤ One Cisco Aironet 1200 access point using IOS-based firmware and interface

➤ One UTP patch cable

➤ Power cable for the access point

➤ Network access through a classroom switch

➤ Access to the instructor's access point, which is connected to the same network infrastructure as your access point, but whose coverage does not overlap with your access point

➤ Completion of the Chapter 2 labs

Estimated completion time: **25 minutes**

5

ACTIVITY

LAB ACTIVITY

1. Connect and power up your team's access point if necessary. Turn on both of your laptops and log in.

2. On both laptops, double-click the **ADU shortcut** on your desktop to open the utility.

3. Click the **Profile Management** tab.

4. Click **New** to create a new profile with the following parameters:

   Profile Name: **Twowap**

   Client Name: Use your computer name, which already should be displayed

5. Click the **Security** tab and make sure **None** is selected.

6. Click the **Advanced** tab. Leave all three wireless modes selected. Leave Infrastructure mode as the network type.

7. Now you will configure the MAC addresses of the access points with which you want to associate. Specifying the access point's MAC address in the client device helps make sure the client will associate with the correct access point if there is more than one with the same SSID. Click the **Preferred AP's** button and enter the MAC address of your access point's radio, as recorded in Step 12 of Lab 2.2 for Access Point 1. (Don't use any periods or dashes.) Ask your instructor for the MAC address of the instructor's access point (kilo-lima), and then enter the address in the Access Point 2 box. Figure 5-1 shows an example of Preferred AP configuration of two MAC addresses. Click **OK**.

8. Click **OK** again to create the Twowap profile.

9. Double-click the **Twowap** profile to activate it. You may lose your wireless connection for a few seconds. Close the ADU utility.

10. Point to the **ADU icon** in the tray. Are both of your laptops connected to your access point using the Twowap profile? _____

    What is your connected speed? _____

    What is your IP address? _____

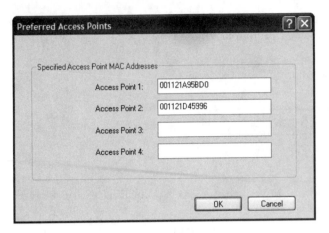

Figure 5-1   Preferred AP example

11. Leave one of your laptops in the room. Take this lab manual and the other laptop and walk slowly toward the instructor's access point.

12. Continue walking slowly toward the instructor's access point while watching the ADU icon in the tray. Do not block the adapter with your hand. At some point the ADU icon will turn gray-white, which indicates complete loss of signal. When this happens, stop and point to the gray-white **ADU icon**. What is displayed in the pop-up window?

_____

13. Continue walking slowly toward the instructor's access point. Eventually, the ADU icon in the tray will turn green. Point to the **ADU icon**. What is displayed in the pop-up window now?

_____

What is your IP address? _____

Access points communicate on the network. That is why your laptop can keep the IP address it received via DHCP, even when reconnecting to the network through a different device.

14. Click **Start**, then right-click **My Computer**. Click **Search**. Click **Computers or People**. Click **A Computer On The Network** and type the name of the laptop (for example, alpha) that you left back in the room with your access point. You should be able to see your laptop via communications between kilo-lima (the instructor's access point) and your access point. Were you successful? _____

15. You should still be in kilo-lima's coverage area. Open the **Aironet Desktop Utility** by double-clicking the shortcut on the desktop.

16. Click the **Current Status** tab if necessary. What is your signal strength?
   _____

   What is your connected speed? _____

   Leave the Aironet Desktop Utility window open.

17. Walk back slowly toward your access point while watching the signal strength indicator. As you begin to lose your signal, you will see the Wireless mode change as the spectrum is scanned for an access point with which to associate. Notice that the client is scanning for an A, B, or G connection because the Twowap profile included those wireless modes.

18. When you get close to your access point, the laptop should reassociate with it. Point to the **ADU icon** in the tray to make sure.

19. Take the laptop back into the room with your access point.

20. Close the Aironet Desktop Utility.

21. Shut down the laptops.

Certification Objectives

Objectives for the CWNA exam:

➤ Identify and apply the processes involved in authentication and association

Review Questions

1. How is signal strength related to mobility?

2. What is the benefit of configuring the MAC address of the access point in the client profile?

3. If your IP address remained the same between access points, why do you think it did?

4. You walked away from one connection in the lab activity and associated with another. Why is this not considered true roaming?

5. When the signal gets weak, the client device starts scanning. Why does this happen?

LAB 5.2 EXPLORING LAYER 2 ROAMING

Objectives

The ability to move between the cells of multiple access points without losing your connectivity is known as roaming. Roaming sometimes is called mobility. There are basically two types of roaming—layer 2 and layer 3. With layer 2 roaming, you roam within a single roaming domain—in other words, within a single subnet. The most common example is when you work on a laptop, close it and walk to a different cell area in the same building, and then open it and resume your work. Layer 2 roaming requires a minimum cell overlap of 20%. Layer 3 roaming involves roaming across subnets and is not part of this lab. Connection-oriented services work best during roaming because any 802.11 data lost during the roaming must be retransmitted by TCP. Data loss during roaming with UDP-based applications can have a noticeable impact on those applications because UDP is connectionless and doesn't provide guaranteed delivery. In a layer 2 roaming scenario, the roaming user can maintain Application layer connectivity within the roaming domain as long as the user's IP address does not change. From the client perspective, there are basically four steps to layer 2 roaming:

1. The client decides to roam.

2. The client decides where to roam via scanning.

3. The client initiates a roam by associating to a new access point.

4. The client resumes existing application sessions.

Roaming algorithms are proprietary and secret—they are not part of the 802.11 standard. But most algorithms depend on signal-to-noise ratios and missed beacons. The layer 2 roaming process, from the perspective of the access point, is basically as follows:

1. The access point determines that the client has roamed away from it.

2. The access point buffers the data destined for the roaming client.

3. The new access point notifies the old access point that the client has successfully roamed.

4. The old access point sends buffered data to the new access point.

5. The old access point updates the MAC address table on the switch.

The purpose of this lab is to investigate the roaming process. The cells between your access point and the instructor's access point (named kilo-lima) overlap sufficiently that roaming can take place. In this lab you will transfer a file using the connection-oriented application FTP while you roam from your access point to your instructor's access point. Although you may detect a slight download interruption during the transfer, the file should transfer successfully.

After completing this lab, you will be able to:

➤ Describe roaming

➤ Understand how roaming is initiated

➤ Understand the parameters necessary for roaming to work

Materials Required

This lab requires the following for each team:

➤ One laptop computer running Windows XP and configured with a Cisco Aironet adapter

➤ One Cisco Aironet 1200 access point using IOS-based firmware and interface

➤ One UTP patch cable

➤ Power cable for the access point

➤ Network access through a classroom switch

➤ Access to the instructor's access point, which is on the same network and whose cell coverage overlaps with your access point's cell coverage at least 20 percent

➤ FTP server software running on the instructor's laptop, with anonymous FTP access to the desktop permitted and a large file named tournament.ssf saved on the desktop

➤ Completion of the Chapter 2 labs

➤ Completion of Lab 5.1

Estimated completion time: 35 minutes

ACTIVITY

1. Connect and power up your team's access point if necessary. Turn on one of your team's laptops and log in. Point to the **ADU icon** in the tray. You should be connected using the **Twowap** profile you created in Lab 5.1. Your laptop is probably still configured to use the Twowap profile, but if it isn't, open the **Aironet Desktop Utility** program and activate the Twowap profile. What is your IP address? _____

2. Take your laptop and this lab manual, then walk slowly away from your access point and toward the instructor's access point named kilo-lima. Watch the **ADU icon** in the tray. The color of the ADU icon may change as the signal-to-noise ratio (SNR) decreases. Green indicates greatest strength. Yellow and red indicate a lesser signal strength and no signal strength, respectively. Because of the overlapping cells of your access point and kilo-lima, you should not lose connectivity.

3. Stop in front of your instructor's access point. Point to the **ADU icon** in the tray. With which access point are you associated? _____

   What is your IP address? _____

   What is your connected speed? _____

   Your laptop should have jumped from your access point to kilo-lima with no loss of signal. What is one factor in making the decision to jump to another access point?

   _____

4. While still in front of your instructor's access point, click **Start**, then click **Run**. Type **cmd** and press **Enter** to open a DOS window. Type **ftp** followed by the FTP server's IP address and press **Enter**. Your instructor will provide you with this IP address. This FTP server is associated with the kilo-lima access point. Log in with the username **anonymous**. Enter your e-mail address as the password.

5. Type **hash** and press **Enter** so you can watch the download as it progresses.

6. Type **get tournament.ssf** and press **Enter**. This large file should begin downloading from the FTP server. Pick up the laptop and walk quickly back toward your own access point. Make sure you are not covering the adapter with your hands. The download may stall, but wait a few seconds and it should finish successfully. An example FTP download is shown in Figure 5-2. To save space, the number of hashes displayed in the figure has been drastically reduced.

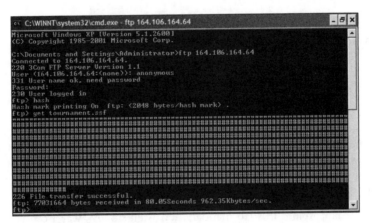

Figure 5-2   FTP download

7. When the download is finished, the throughput in kilobytes per second should be indicated in the DOS window. What is the reported throughput in kilobytes per second? _____

8. To open the Windows calculator, click **Start** and then click **Run**. Type **calc** and then press **Enter**. Convert the throughput you recorded in Step 7 to megabits per second by multiplying by 8 bits/byte and then dividing by 1000. What is the reported throughput in megabits per second? _____

9. If you are using an "a" or "g" radio, you may think you are experiencing 54 Mbps when communicating wirelessly. In reality, the best you can hope to achieve is 50 percent or 60 percent of the rated bandwidth. When roaming, this percentage will be further reduced. Calculate the percentage of the rated bandwidth you experienced during the download by dividing the reported throughput recorded in Step 8 by the rated bandwidth of your connection.

_____

10. Type **quit** at the ftp prompt in the DOS window, then close the DOS window.

11. Open Internet Explorer and browse to your access point using its IP address, which you configured in Step 15 of Lab 2.2. You will be prompted for a user-name and password. The username is **administrator**. The password is **Cisco**.

12. Click **Event Log** in the browser window and scroll through the events. You should see entries for your laptop as it became associated, then deauthenticated and deassociated as you walked in and out of range of your access point.

13. Close any open windows. Shut down the laptops.

Certification Objectives

Objectives for the CWNA exam:

➤ Identify and apply the processes involved in authentication and association

Review Questions

1. What is the difference between layer 2 roaming and layer 3 roaming?

2. How much cell overlap is required for layer 2 roaming to work?

3. Why should we expect a lower throughput rate when roaming?

4. The decision to roam from one access point to another largely depends on the signal-to-noise ratio. True or False?

5. How does the client know where to roam?

LAB 5.3 CONFIGURING POWER MANAGEMENT OPTIONS AVAILABLE WITH CISCO'S 802.11 A/B/G CLIENT ADAPTER

Objectives

Most wireless client utilities include various power management options. Power management is important when communicating with devices such as laptops that are not connected to a power source at all times. The Aironet Desktop Utility included with your Cisco 802.11 a/b/g wireless adapter provides three power management modes. The default is CAM—continuous aware mode. CAM keeps the client adapter powered up continuously so there is little lag in message response time. This mode consumes the most power but offers the highest throughput. In fast power save polling mode (FastPSP), the adapter switches between powering the wireless adapter on and off, depending on an algorithm and network traffic. When receiving a large amount of frames, a FastPSP mode adapter will remain in CAM until all frames have been received. Finally, the a/b/g adapter can be placed in maximum power save polling mode (MaxPSP). This mode conserves the most power but offers the lowest throughput. The wireless adapter sleeps, but wakes up periodically to see if any messages are waiting for it.

The purpose of this lab is to configure the various power management modes via the Aironet Desktop Utility and see the effects these modes have on the wireless adapter.

After completing this lab, you will be able to:

➤ Explain the difference in practical terms between the various power management options available with the Cisco a/b/g adapter

Materials Required

This lab requires the following for each team:

➤ Two laptop computers running Windows XP and configured with a Cisco Aironet adapter

➤ One Cisco Aironet 1200 access point using IOS-based firmware and interface

➤ One UTP patch cable

➤ Power cable for the access point

➤ Completion of the Chapter 2 labs

Estimated completion time: **20 minutes**

ACTIVITY

1. Connect and power up your team's access point if necessary. Turn on both of your laptops and log in.

2. Open the **ADU** program by double-clicking its icon on the desktop.

3. Change to the Infrastructure Mode profile if necessary by clicking the **Profile Management** tab and then double-clicking the **Infrastructure Mode** profile.

4. With the Infrastructure Mode profile selected, click the **Modify** button. Next, click the **Advanced** tab. What is the default power save mode for your adapter? _____

5. On only one of the laptops, change to **FastPSP mode**. Click **OK**.

6. On both laptops, click the **Diagnostics** tab and then click the **Advanced Statistics** button. What differences do you see between the CAM laptop and the FastPSP laptop?

   _____

   Do you notice any difference in LED activity on the adapters?

   _____

7. On the FastPSP mode laptop, click **OK** to close the Advanced Statistics window. Click the **Profile Management** tab, click the **Modify** button, and then click the **Advanced** tab.

8. Change the FastPSP mode laptop to **Max PSP** mode. Click **OK**, then click the **Diagnostics** tab and the **Advanced Statistics** button. Once again, compare the activity on-screen and the LED activity on the adapters.

   _____

   Can you tell that Max PSP mode conserves the most power?

   _____

9. On both laptops, click **OK**, then click the **Profile Management** tab and double-click your **Ad Hoc Mode** profile to select it.

10. Click the **Modify** button and then click the **Advanced** tab. Can you adjust the power save mode on this adapter when you are in ad hoc mode?

    _____

11. On both laptops, click **OK** and then double-click the **Infrastructure Mode** profile to select it.

12. On the laptop configured for Max PSP mode, click the **Modify** button and then click the **Advanced** tab. Change Max PSP mode to **CAM**. Click **OK**.

13. Close any open windows. Shut down the laptops.

5

Certification Objectives

Objectives for the CWNA exam:

➤ Understand the implications of power management features for wireless LANs

Review Questions

1. What three power options are available with the Cisco Aironet a/b/g wireless adapter?

2. Which mode offers the best throughput and why?

3. Which mode prolongs the laptop battery the most and why?

4. How would you decide which mode to use for your wireless client?

5. Which mode do you think would be best for a wireless desktop computer? Why?

LAB 5.4 CONFIGURING SHARED KEY AUTHENTICATION

Objectives

The 802.11 standard specifies two methods of authentication—open and shared key. Open authentication is the default on Cisco devices and is considered "null authentication," because there really is no authentication involved. Using open authentication, any device with the same SSID as the access point can authenticate and associate to it. The other supported authentication method is shared key authentication. With shared key authentication configured, your client will not be authenticated or associated by the access point until it encrypts, with a WEP key, a plaintext challenge sent by the access point. The current version of WEP supports two key sizes: 40-bit, which is the same as 64-bit, and 104-bit, which is the same as 128-bit. The extra 24 bits that may or may not be included in the reported bit strength is due to an initialization vector, which is part of the WEP security standard. A 40-bit WEP key requires 10 hexadecimal digits, and a 128-bit WEP key requires 26 hexadecimal digits. Using shared key authentication, the unencrypted challenge and the encrypted challenge are both transmitted. The transmission can be monitored, and an intruder who could calculate the WEP key by comparing the unencrypted and encrypted text strings would be able to decipher all communications transmitted with that key. Because of this weakness, shared key is considered less secure than open authentication, although neither is considered to be a complete security solution. The purpose of this lab is to become familiar with shared key authentication and learn how to configure it.

In this lab, you will use HyperTerminal and the command-line interface to remove open authentication and configure shared key authentication. You will then create a new profile on your laptop so you can communicate using this authentication type. Finally, you will reconfigure the access point for open authentication.

After completing this lab, you will be able to:

➤ Configure shared key authentication on a Cisco 1200 series access point using the command-line interface

➤ Configure a shared key profile on your laptops so they can authenticate to your access point using shared key authentication

Materials Required

This lab requires the following for each team:

➤ Two laptop computers running Windows XP and configured with a Cisco Aironet adapter

➤ One Cisco Aironet 1200 access point using IOS-based firmware and interface

➤ One console (rollover) cable

➤ One DB-9-to-RJ-45 adapter (may not be necessary if console cable has one DB-9 end)

➤ Power cable for the access point

➤ Completion of the Chapter 2 labs

Estimated completion time: **35 minutes**

LAB ACTIVITY

ACTIVITY

1. Turn on both team laptops and log in.

2. Point to the **ADU icon** in the tray to make sure you are connected to your own access point using the Infrastructure Mode profile. The SSID should be your team name with "wap" appended to it (for example, alpha-bravowap). If this is not the case, double-click the **Aironet Desktop Utility** shortcut on the desktop to open the program. Click the **Profile Management** tab and double-click **Infrastructure Mode**. In a few seconds, you should connect to your access point. Close the ADU utility.

3. Disconnect your access point from the switch if it is connected.

4. Attach a DB-9-to-RJ-45 adapter to the COM1 port on the back of one of your laptops. Connect a rollover cable to the DB-9 connector. Attach the other end of the cable to the console port on the back of your team's access point. If you have a rollover cable with one DB-9 end, you will not need the DB-9-to-RJ-45 adapter.

5. If necessary, turn on the access point by plugging it in.

6. Click **Start**, point to **All Programs**, point to **Accessories**, point to **Communications**, point to **HyperTerminal**, and click the connection you created in Lab 2.2. If you didn't save or create a connection, follow Steps 4 through 8 in Lab 2.2 to create a new connection.

7. Text now appears in the HyperTerminal window. If text does not appear, press **Enter**. Eventually, the ap> prompt displays.

8. Type **enable** and press **Enter**. You are prompted for a password, which for this particular IOS is Cisco, and is case sensitive. Type **Cisco** and press **Enter**. Notice that the prompt changes to ap#. This is privileged mode, which also is known as enable mode.

9. Type **show run** and press **Enter**. The current configuration of the access point displays. Press the Spacebar to scroll through the output as necessary. What is the name of the SSID you configured? _____

   What type of authentication is configured for this SSID? _____

10. Using the following commands, configure your access point to use shared key authentication. Your input may be interrupted by messages during this process. You may need to press **Enter** at various points to clear messages.

    conf t [Enter]

    int dot11radio0 [Enter]

    ssid [your SSID name here] [Enter]

    no auth open

    auth shared

    exit

    encryption key 1 size 40 0123456789

    encryption mode ciphers wep40

    Ctrl+Z

    [Enter] (to clear messages)

    show run [Enter]

11. Use the Spacebar to scroll through the configuration and to verify that shared key authentication is configured for your SSID. Minimize the HyperTerminal window.

12. On both laptops, point to the **ADU icon** in the tray. Notice that you have lost your wireless connection because your Infrastructure Mode profile is active and it is configured for open authentication. You need a client profile that uses shared key authentication. If necessary, open the **Aironet Desktop Utility** from the desktop shortcut on both laptops.

13. Create a new profile named **Shared Key Authentication**. Configure your SSID name (for example, alpha-bravowap) in the SSID1: text box. On the **Security** tab, select **Pre-Shared key (static WEP)**, and then click the **Configure** button.

14. Click in the **WEP Key 1:** text box and enter **0123456789**, which is the same WEP key you configured on the access point. Make sure that **Hexadecimal** and a key size of **40** are selected. Click **OK.**

15. Click the **Advanced** tab and select **Shared** for the 802.11 Authentication Mode.

16. Click **OK** to return to the Profile Management window.

17. Double-click the **Shared Key Authentication** profile to activate it. Within a few seconds, you should be reconnected.

18. Now you will remove the shared key from your access point. Return to the HyperTerminal window and enter the following commands:

    conf t [Enter]

    int dot11radio0 [Enter]

    ssid [your SSID name here] [Enter]

    no auth shared

    auth open

    exit

    no encryption key 1 size 40 0123456789

    no encryption mode ciphers wep40

    Ctrl+Z

    [Enter] (to clear messages)

    show run [Enter] (Press the Spacebar to scroll through the remaining output; make sure your access point is configured for open authentication with no encryption)

    copy run start [Enter] (Press **Enter** again to accept the default "startup-config")

19. Close the HyperTerminal window. Point to the **ADU icon** in the tray. You should have lost connectivity. Why did you lose connectivity?

_____

20. Return to the **Profile Management** tab in the **Aironet Desktop Utility** program. Double-click the **Infrastructure Mode** profile to activate it. Did you reconnect? _____

21. Close all windows and shut down the laptops. Power down your access point.

Certification Objectives

Objectives for the CWNA exam:

➤ Identify and apply the processes involved in authentication and association

Review Questions

1. What are the two authentication methods required by the 802.11 standard?

2. Which of these two authentication methods is considered more secure, and why?

3. What are the two WEP key strengths currently supported by 802.11?

4. Why did you lose connectivity in the lab activity when you configured your access point for shared key authentication?

5. List the WEP key strengths with their corresponding required number of hexadecimal digits.

LAB 5.5 INVESTIGATING THE RELATIONSHIP BETWEEN FRAGMENTATION AND PERFORMANCE

Objectives

Wireless frames have a maximum size of 2346 bytes. Beyond that, the 802.11 specification mandates that the frames will be fragmented. With some systems, fragmentation occurs at 1518 bytes because that is the maximum size of wired Ethernet frames, and the access point is usually attached to the wired Ethernet network. Every frame that is sent on a wireless network must have a header and a frame check sequence (FCS) trailer. The FCS is also known as the CRC, which stands for Cyclical Redundancy Check. In addition to the header and trailer, each wireless frame must be acknowledged, because there is no collision detection mechanism on wireless networks. Wireless systems use CSMA/CA rather than CSMA/CD. The "CA" stands for collision avoidance, and the acknowledgment (ACK) frames are part of the collision avoidance scheme. It makes sense to use the maximum frame size in order to avoid the additional headers, trailers, and ACKs, which become overhead on your wireless network and reduce your data throughput. The problem is that bigger frames have a greater chance of colliding, so as fragment size increases, your network may be adversely affected due to retransmissions. Part of a wireless network administrator's job is understanding fragmentation and how it affects network performance. Very often, the size beyond which frames are fragmented, known as the fragmentation threshold, will have to be tweaked. The purpose of this lab is to change the fragmentation threshold setting and observe the affects on the wireless network using AiroPeek. AiroPeek is a very effective network analyzer for 802.11 networks. It is expensive to purchase but the demo version is free.

In this lab you will configure various fragmentation thresholds on your access point and use AiroPeek to monitor performance.

After completing this lab, you will be able to:

➤ Configure different fragmentation thresholds

➤ Learn the value of using network analyzers to measure performance parameters

➤ Understand how manipulating fragmentation threshold values can improve performance on your wireless network

Materials Required

This lab requires the following for each team:

➤ Two laptop computers running Windows XP and configured with a Cisco Aironet adapter

➤ One Cisco Aironet 1200 access point using IOS-based firmware and interface

➤ One UTP patch cable

➤ Power cable for the access point

➤ Network access through a classroom switch

➤ Completion of the Chapter 2 labs

Estimated completion time: **75 minutes**

LAB ACTIVITY

ACTIVITY

This lab involves the use of a Web site that may have changed since the writing of this lab. Therefore, the exact link names and locations may have changed.

1. Power up your access point and connect it to the classroom switch if necessary. Turn on both laptops and log in.

2. Point to the **ADU icon** in the tray. You should be connected to your access point using the Infrastructure Mode profile. If you are not using the Infrastructure Mode profile, open the **Aironet Desktop Utility** by double-clicking the desktop shortcut. Click the **Profile Management** tab and double-click the **Infrastructure Mode** profile to activate it. In a few seconds, you should connect to your access point.

3. You will download and install AiroPeek on one laptop. Open Internet Explorer and browse to **www.wildpackets.com** on one laptop. Point to **Products** and then click **Demos**.

4. Check **AiroPeek SE** (not the NX version), then scroll down and fill in the contact information. The e-mail address you give will be the one to which the product link is sent, so don't use a fake e-mail address. Use an e-mail address that you can access online. Answer the survey question, then scroll down if necessary and click **Submit**.

5. Agree to the license information by clicking **I agree to the terms above**.

6. Access your Web-based e-mail account used to request AiroPeek. You should have a message from WildPackets. Open the e-mail and then click the embedded link.

7. Select **HTTP Download** and save the file to your desktop.

8. Close all windows and double-click **apwdemo** from your desktop to begin installation. Click **Run** if you get a security warning.

9. Click **Setup**. Click **OK** in the warning window and install the demo, accepting all defaults. If prompted, enter any username and company name you want. Click **Finish**.

10. Once you click **Finish**, a window notifies you that you must install a special driver in order for AiroPeek to work. This is true, but the driver is not in the list presented, so close the window.

11. Click **Start**, point to **All Programs**, and then click **WildPackets AiroPeek Demo**. Read the demo limitations window and then click **OK**.

12. The program should start and the Monitor Options window should appear. If it doesn't, click the **Monitor** menu and then click **Select Monitor Adapter**. Click the **Cisco Wireless Adapter**. Click **OK**. Click **OK** again if you get the driver warning.

13. Click **Help** on the menu bar, then click **Readme**. Scroll down and click the link for supported network adapters.

14. Scroll down to the **802.11 Multi-band cards** section.

15. Click **New Atheros driver 3.0.0.111a** for the Cisco Aironet 802.11 a/b/g adapter.

16. Scroll down and click the download link to download the driver. Save it to the desktop.

17. Right-click your **wireless connection icon** in the tray and click **Open Network Connections**.

18. Right-click the **Cisco Wireless Adapter** and click **Properties**.

19. Click the **Configure** button.

20. Click the **Driver** tab and then click the **Update Driver** button.

21. Click **No, not this time**, then click **Next**.

22. Select **Install from a list or specific location**. Click **Next**.

23. Click **Don't Search**, and then click **Next**.

24. Click **Have Disk**.

25. Browse to find the **Atheros3.0** folder. Double-click the filename, which is **net5211.inf**. Click **OK**. Click **Next**.

26. When you see a warning regarding Windows Logo testing, click **Continue Anyway**.

27. Click **Finish** and restart your laptop, even if not prompted. Make sure you can still connect to the Internet. If you cannot connect, you most likely have a driver problem, and you should return to the **Driver** tab on the Cisco Wireless Adapter Properties window and click **Rollback Driver**. Then try the driver update process again.

28. On the non-AiroPeek laptop, open Internet Explorer. Browse to your access point using the IP address you recorded in Step 15 of Lab 2.2. Log in with the username **administrator**. The password is **Cisco**.

29. Click **Network Interfaces**, then click **Radio0-802.11G**. (Your radio interface may have a slightly different name.) Click the **Settings** tab.

5

30. Scroll down to the **Data Rates** section. Click the **Default** button to make sure **Default** is selected before continuing.

31. Scroll to the **Default Radio Channel** section. Your access point should be configured to use the channel specified in Lab 4.4, Table 4-5. If it is not, use the list box to change to the correct channel for your access point. What channel are you using? _____

32. Scroll down to the **Fragmentation Threshold** information. What is the default fragmentation threshold for your access point? _____

    In terms of frame sizes, what does this fragmentation threshold correspond to?
    _____

    Scroll to the bottom of the page and click **Apply**, then click **OK**.

33. Changing the channel may cause you to lose connectivity. If this happens, open the **Aironet Desktop Utility** program and click the **Profile Management** tab. Click the **Scan** button, then click **Refresh**. You should reconnect. Click **OK** and close the Aironet Desktop Utility program.

34. Minimize the Cisco IOS Web browser window and open a second Internet Explorer window. Navigate to **www.wgst.com**. Click **Listen Live**, then click **Click here to launch our stream**. If asked to play using Internet Explorer, click **Yes**. If prompted, click to install the latest version of **Media Player** and install it using the default settings. Eventually, Media Player should open and begin streaming audio. It may take a few minutes to hear audio if WGST is broadcasting commercials. Don't continue until you hear streaming audio. Adjust the volume as necessary to avoid disturbing the other teams.

35. On the AiroPeek laptop, click **Start**, point to **All Programs**, and then click **WildPackets AiroPeek Demo** to open the program. Click **OK**. You will lose your connectivity while AiroPeek is open. This is normal, and happens because your wireless adapter is in passive mode sniffing traffic. It cannot sniff and transmit at the same time.

36. Click **File** on the menu bar, then click **New** to begin creating a new capture in AiroPeek.

37. On the **802.11** tab, change the Number: field to reflect the channel you recorded in Step 31. Click **OK**.

38. On the **Filters** tab, click the check box to select **802.11 Data**. Click **OK**. On the non-AiroPeek laptop, you still should be streaming audio.

39. In AiroPeek, click the **Start Capture** button. The demo will capture up to 250 packets for up to 30 seconds.

40. Soon, the AiroPeek capture will end. Click **OK**. Also, the Monitor Statistics function will end at some point. When you see the notification window, click **OK** and continue with the lab. If the streaming stopped during the capture, redo the capture.

41. In AiroPeek, click the **Graphs** tab at the bottom of the capture window. This window charts percentages for various packet size ranges. Figure 5-3 shows example output using the Graphs tab. Record the size ranges and their percentages for the three largest percentages in Table 5-1.

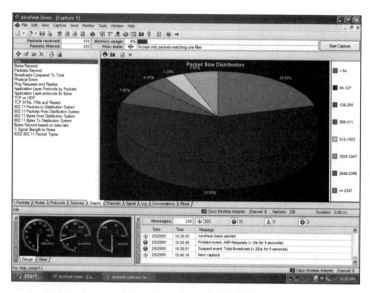

5

Figure 5-3   Example AiroPeek output using the Graphs tab

Table 5-1   Packet size ranges for 2346-byte fragmentation threshold

Packet Size Range for 2346-byte Fragmentation	Percentage

42. Click the **Summary** tab at the bottom of the capture window. This window summarizes the types and numbers of packets. Figure 5-4 shows example output using AiroPeek's Summary tab. In the toolbar, you should see Packets Received and Packets Filtered. How many packets were received in the 30-second capture? _____

Look in the Statistics window. What was the average utilization in Kbps? _____

How many total errors were logged? _____

Close the capture window, but not the AiroPeek program.

43. On the streaming laptop, leave audio streaming on but return to the Cisco IOS Web browser window.

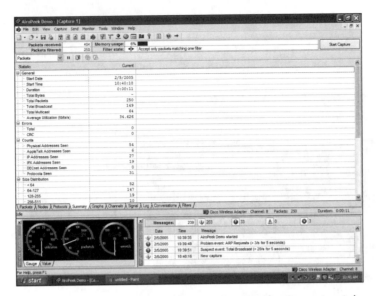

Figure 5-4   Example AiroPeek output using the Summary tab

44. You still should see the **Settings** tab for the **Radio0–802.11G** radio. If not, navigate to that window.

45. Scroll down to the **Fragmentation Threshold** text box. Change the fragmentation threshold to **1518** bytes. Click **Apply**, then click **OK**. Make sure you still are streaming on the Internet Explorer laptop.

46. Create a new capture in AiroPeek using the correct channel as recorded in Step 31, and a filter on Data packets as before. Click **Start Capture**, and when the capture is done, return to the **Graphs** tab and enter your findings in Table 5-2.

Table 5-2   Packet size ranges for 1518-byte fragmentation threshold

Packet Size Range for 1518-byte Fragmentation	Percentage

47. Click the **Summary** tab at the bottom of the capture window. How many packets were received in the 30-second capture? _____

What was the average utilization in Kbps? _____

How many total errors were logged? _____

Close the capture window.

48. Repeat Steps 43 through 46 using a fragmentation threshold of **256**. Record your findings in Table 5-3.

Table 5-3 Packet size ranges for 256-byte fragmentation threshold

Packet Size Range for 256-byte Fragmentation	Percentage

49. Click the **Summary** tab at the bottom of the capture window. How many packets were received in the 30-second capture? _____

    What was the average utilization in Kbps? _____

    How many total errors were logged? _____

    Close the capture window.

50. Record all of your data from the Summary tab in Table 5-4 for easy comparison:

Table 5-4 Fragmentation threshold comparison from Summary tab

Fragmentation Threshold	Number of Packets Received	Average Utilization	Total Errors
2346			
1518			
256			

51. According to the packet size tables, what happened to the percentage of packets sized 256 to 511 bytes as the fragmentation threshold was reduced?

    _____

    Does this make sense? _____

    Why or why not?

    _____

52. According to Table 5-4, what was the effect of reducing the fragmentation threshold on the number of packets received?

    _____

    What was the effect of reducing the fragmentation threshold on errors?

    _____

    Do your results support or refute the hypothesis that smaller fragments will reduce collisions and errors up to a point, but at some point will create enough overhead that performance will be degraded? _____

    Which fragmentation setting would you recommend on your system if audio streaming frequently is used? _____

53. Reconfigure the **fragmentation threshold** to the default, which is **2346** bytes, using Steps 43 through 46 as your guide.

54. Close all windows and shut down the laptops.

Certification Objectives

Objectives for the CWNA exam:

➤ Specify the modes of operation involved in the movement of data traffic across wireless LANs

Review Questions

1. What is the maximum size of an 802.11 wireless frame?

2. Why does CSMA/CA have more overhead than CSMA/CD?

3. What is the relationship between wireless frame size and probability of collisions?

4. What is the advantage of using relatively smaller wireless frames?

5. What is the advantage of using relatively larger wireless frames?

CHAPTER SIX

PLANNING AND DEPLOYING A WIRELESS LAN

Labs included in this chapter

➤ Lab 6.1 Measuring Ad Hoc Mode Throughput

➤ Lab 6.2 Measuring Infrastructure Mode Throughput Using the Cisco 1200 Series Access Point

➤ Lab 6.3 Configuring the Cisco 1200 Series Access Point for Repeater Mode and Measuring Throughput

➤ Lab 6.4 Measuring Infrastructure Mode Throughput Using the Linksys Wireless Router

➤ Lab 6.5 Determining if Going Wireless is Worthwhile

CWNA Exam Objectives	
Objective	**Lab**
Recognize the concepts associated with wireless LAN service sets	6.1, 6.2, 6.3, 6.4

Lab 6.5 does not map directly to objectives on the exam. However, it teaches a skill that is valuable to wireless networking professionals.

LAB 6.1 MEASURING AD HOC MODE THROUGHPUT

Objectives

It is important to note that a wireless access point, although primarily a Data Link layer device, operates like a hub. The bandwidth is shared and the actual throughput is much less than you might expect. 802.11 systems use CSMA/CA for media access rather than CSMA/CD, which is used for Ethernet. The "CA" stands for collision avoidance, while "CD" stands for collision detection. Collision avoidance is used because wireless devices have no way to detect a collision. One of the reasons for the lower than expected throughput is the way CSMA/CA operates. There is much more overhead associated with CSMA/CA than with CSMA/CD. In addition, this overhead increases as the number of users accessing the network simultaneously increases—just like it does when using a hub. In general, the more devices a wireless frame must pass through, the lower the throughput. So, we would expect that transferring a file using ad hoc mode would be more efficient than transferring the same file using one or more access points in infrastructure or repeater mode. When devices communicate in ad hoc mode, which is without an access point, the configuration is called an Independent Basic Service Set (IBSS). When devices communicate in infrastructure mode using a single access point, the configuration is called a Basic Service Set (BSS). When devices communicate in infrastructure mode, roaming between multiple access points, the configuration is called an Extended Service Set (ESS). The purpose of this lab is to measure the throughput realized when transferring a file from one peer to another using ad hoc mode. The results can be compared to the throughput measurements from Lab 5.2, the layer 2 roaming lab, as well as with other labs in this chapter that involve transferring the same file in infrastructure mode and repeater mode. In this lab your team will use ad hoc mode to transfer a file using FTP.

After completing this lab, you will be able to:

➤ Measure and describe the throughput realized in an ad hoc mode file transfer

➤ Understand the difference between an IBSS, a BSS, and an ESS

Materials Required

This lab requires the following for each team:

➤ Two laptop computers running Windows XP and configured with a Cisco Aironet adapter

➤ 3cs117.zip file (free FTP program provided by instructor)

➤ Tournament.ssf file (file provided by instructor)

➤ WinZip program installed on laptops

➤ Completion of the Chapter 2 labs

ACTIVITY

1. Power down your team's access point if necessary. Turn on your team's laptops and log in.

2. Point to the **ADU** icon in the tray. You should be connected to your ad hoc network, which has the same SSID as your team name—for example, alpha-bravo. If you are connected to your ad hoc network, skip to Step 3. If you are not connected in ad hoc mode, open the **Aironet Desktop Utility** and switch to your Ad hoc Mode profile by double-clicking the profile name.

3. Choose one of the team laptops to be an FTP server. The other will be the FTP client. What is the name of the server? _____

   What is the name of the client? _____

4. On the FTP server laptop, copy the compressed **3cs117.zip** file and the **tournament.ssf** file to the desktop. Your instructor will provide you with these files.

5. On the FTP server, double-click the compressed **3cs117.zip** file to open it. Double-click the **Setup.exe** file to install the program. Accept all default settings. Open the program, if necessary, by clicking **Start**, pointing to **All Programs**, pointing to **3CServer**, and then clicking **3CServer**. Make sure the FTP server button is on.

6. On the server, click the **Setup** button, then click the **FTP Configuration** tab. Make sure all of the **Anonymous Access** check boxes are checked. If necessary, change the **Anonymous Upload/Download** directory to the **Desktop** using the **Browse** button. Click **OK**. The server software should still be running on the desktop.

7. You will do the following steps on the FTP client. Click **Start** and then click **Run**. Type **cmd** in the text box and press **Enter** to open a DOS window.

8. Type **ftp** and then follow the command with a **space** and the **IP address** (or name) of the FTP server. You can find the IP address by pointing to the ADU icon in the tray of the server. Press **Enter** to open an FTP session with the server.

9. Log in as **anonymous** and enter your e-mail address for the password.

10. Type **dir** to see a listing of files on the FTP server. You should see the tournament.ssf file, which is approximately 77 MB.

11. Type **hash** and press **Enter**. This will allow you to watch the download as a series of hash marks in the DOS window.

12. Type **get tournament.ssf** and press **Enter**. The file should begin downloading from the FTP server.

13. When the download is finished, the throughput in kilobytes per second should be indicated in the DOS window. What is the reported throughput in kilobytes per second? _____

14. To open the Windows calculator, click **Start**, then click **Run**. Type **calc**, then press **Enter**. Convert the throughput in kilobytes per second recorded in Step 13 to megabits per second (Mbps) by multiplying by 8 bits/byte and then dividing by 1000. What is the reported throughput in Mbps?

    _____

15. Calculate the percentage of the rated bandwidth you experienced during the download by dividing the reported throughput recorded in Step 14 by the rated bandwidth of your connection. If you are using the 802.11g standard, the rated bandwidth is 54 Mbps.

    _____

16. If you completed Lab 5.2, what was the percentage of rated bandwidth, in Mbps, you experienced while transferring the same file while roaming? This value was recorded in Step 9 of Lab 5.2.

    _____

17. Type **quit** at the ftp prompt in the DOS window, then close the DOS window.

18. On the FTP server, close 3CServer.

19. Shut down your laptops.

Certification Objectives

Objectives for the CWNA exam:

➤ Recognize the concepts associated with wireless LAN service sets

Review Questions

1. What is the advantage of using the hash command when downloading a file using FTP?

2. What units does FTP use to report throughput?

3. Theoretically speaking, why should communicating in ad hoc mode be more efficient than communicating in infrastructure mode?

4. If you completed Lab 5.2 as well as this lab, how did transferring the file through two access points while roaming compare to transferring the same file in ad hoc mode?

5. How meaningful is the term "rated bandwidth" when talking to wireless users about the kind of performance they can expect on the new wireless LAN?

6

LAB 6.2 MEASURING INFRASTRUCTURE MODE THROUGHPUT USING THE CISCO 1200 SERIES ACCESS POINT

Objectives

In Lab 6.1, you saw that only 40 percent or less of the available bandwidth can be used for data transfer when communicating in ad hoc mode. Most wireless networks use access points in either a Basic Service Set or an Extended Service Set configuration. Both of these configurations use infrastructure mode. Infrastructure mode involves a frame contending twice for the medium. The frame contends for bandwidth from the source node to the access point and then again from the access point to the destination node. This process typically reduces throughput by another 50 percent. The purpose of this lab is to measure the resulting throughput from downloading a file from one laptop to another through an access point.

In this lab you will transfer the same file you transferred in Lab 6.1, but you will use infrastructure mode. The throughput measured will be compared to the ad hoc throughput measured in the previous lab, as well as to the roaming throughput if you completed Lab 5.2.

After completing this lab, you will be able to:

➤ Measure and describe the throughput realized in an infrastructure mode file transfer

➤ Understand how infrastructure mode transfer differs from ad hoc mode transfer

Materials Required

This lab requires the following for each team:

➤ Two laptop computers running Windows XP and configured with a Cisco Aironet adapter

➤ One Cisco Aironet 1200 access point using IOS-based firmware and interface

➤ One UTP patch cable

➤ Power cable for the access point

➤ 3cs117.zip file (free FTP program provided by instructor)

➤ Tournament.ssf file (file provided by instructor)

➤ Completion of the Chapter 2 labs

➤ Completion of Lab 6.1

Estimated completion time: **35 minutes**

LAB ACTIVITY

ACTIVITY

1. Connect and power up your team's access point if necessary. Turn on your team's laptops and log in. Point to the **ADU** icon in the tray. If you are using ad hoc mode instead of infrastructure mode, open the **Aironet Desktop Utility**, click the **Profile Management** tab, and double-click your **Infrastructure Mode** profile to activate it. You should be connected to your access point before continuing.

2. On the FTP server laptop, click **Start**, point to **All Programs**, point to **3CServer**, and then click **3CServer**. Make sure the FTP server button is on.

3. You will do the following steps on the FTP client laptop. Click **Start**, then click **Run**. Type **cmd** in the text box and press **Enter** to open a DOS window.

4. Type **ftp** and then follow the command with a **space** and the **IP address** (or name) of the laptop that is serving as the FTP server. Press **Enter** to open an FTP session with the server.

5. Log in as **anonymous** and enter your e-mail address for the password.

6. Type **dir** to see a listing of files on the FTP server. You should see the tournament.ssf file, which is approximately 77 MB.

7. Type **hash** and press **Enter**. This will allow you to watch the download as a series of hash marks in the DOS window.

8. Type **get tournament.ssf** and press **Enter**. The file should begin downloading from the FTP server.

9. When the download is finished, the throughput in kilobytes per second should be indicated in the DOS window. What is the reported throughput in kilobytes per second? _____

10. To open the Windows calculator, click **Start**, then click **Run**. Type **calc**, then press **Enter**. Convert the throughput in kilobytes per second recorded in Step 9 to megabits per second (Mbps) by multiplying by 8 bits/byte and then dividing by 1000. What is the reported throughput in Mbps?

_____

11. Calculate the percentage of the rated bandwidth you experienced during the download by dividing the reported throughput recorded in Step 10 by the rated bandwidth of your connection. If you are using the 802.11g standard, the rated bandwidth is 54 Mbps.

_____

12. What was the percentage of rated bandwidth, in Mbps, you experienced while transferring the same file while roaming? This value was recorded in Step 9 of Lab 5.2.

_____

13. What was the percentage of rated bandwidth, in Mbps, you experienced while transferring the same file in ad hoc mode? This value was recorded in Step 15 of Lab 6.1.

_____

14. Type **quit** at the ftp prompt in the DOS window, then close the DOS window.

15. On the FTP server, close 3CServer.

16. Shut down the laptops.

Certification Objectives

Objectives for the CWNA exam:

➤ Recognize the concepts associated with wireless LAN service sets

Review Questions

1. How did infrastructure mode throughput compare to ad hoc mode throughput?

2. How did BSS throughput in this lab compare with ESS throughput in Lab 5.2?

3. How many times does a wireless frame contend for bandwidth in infrastructure mode compared to ad hoc mode?

4. The overhead associated with CSMA/CA reduces total throughput by approximately the same percentage, regardless of the number of devices the wireless frame must pass through. True or False?

5. Theoretically, roaming across an ESS introduces more overhead than communicating within a BSS. True or False?

Lab 6.3 Configuring the Cisco 1200 Series Access Point for Repeater Mode and Measuring Throughput

Objectives

Throughout this lab manual, you have been using the Cisco 1200 series access point in its most common manifestation—access mode. Access mode is also known as root mode. This means the access point is authenticating and associating client devices so they can access the wired network. Many access points, including the 1200, can also be configured for repeater mode. In repeater mode, the access point is not wired to the network. Its purpose is to connect clients that are out of range of the root mode access point and that would otherwise be unable to gain access to the wired network. The repeater accepts clients as an access point, then associates with the upstream root access point as a client itself. The root access point is considered the parent of the repeater access point. In order for repeater mode to work correctly, there must be approximately 50 percent cell overlap between the root access point and the repeater. By default, repeaters associate with the root access point that has the strongest signal, but specifying the MAC address of the wired access point directs the repeater to associate with a specific root device. The purpose of this lab is to investigate repeater mode and to measure and compare the throughput using a repeater versus basic root mode infrastructure throughput. You will see that using repeater mode is not advisable unless absolutely necessary. In this lab you will configure your Cisco 1200 for repeater mode and direct your repeater to associate with the instructor's access point, kilo-lima, which will be the root mode device. You will then transfer the same file transferred in Labs 5.2, 6.1, and 6.2 and compare the throughput results. Because repeaters have to repeat every frame, you should expect an additional 50 percent loss in throughput as compared to your basic infrastructure mode throughput (BSS).

After completing this lab, you will be able to:

➤ Measure and describe the throughput realized in a repeater mode file transfer

➤ Understand how repeater mode drastically reduces throughput as compared to basic infrastructure mode

Materials Required

This lab requires the following for each team:

➤ One laptop computer running Windows XP and configured with a Cisco Aironet adapter

➤ One Cisco Aironet 1200 access point using IOS-based firmware and interface

➤ One console (rollover) cable

➤ One DB-9-to-RJ-45 adapter (may not be necessary if console cable has one DB-9 end)

➤ Power cable for the access point

➤ 3cs117.zip file (free FTP program provided by instructor)

➤ Tournament.ssf file (file provided by instructor)

➤ The instructor's access point kilo-lima configured with the SSID kilo-limawap

➤ Completion of the Chapter 2 labs

➤ Completion of Labs 6.1 and 6.2

6

Estimated completion time: **50 minutes**

LAB ACTIVITY

ACTIVITY

1. Refer to Figure 6-1 for the configuration of this lab. Turn on one laptop and log in. Power down and disconnect your access point from the switch if necessary.

2. Attach a DB-9-to-RJ-45 adapter to the COM1 port on the back of the laptop. Connect a rollover cable to the DB-9 connector. Attach the other end of the cable to the console port on the back of your team's access point.

3. Turn on the access point by plugging it in. It should not be connected to the switch.

4. Click **Start**, point to **All Programs**, point to **Accessories**, point to **Communications**, and then click **HyperTerminal**. Click the connection you created in Lab 2.2. If you didn't save your connection from Lab 2.2, or if you used the other laptop with HyperTerminal, you can create a new connection. Follow Steps 4 through 9 of Lab 2.2 to create a new connection, if necessary.

5. Text appears in the HyperTerminal window. If text does not appear, press **Enter**. Eventually, the ap> prompt displays.

6. Type **enable** and press **Enter**. When prompted for a password, type **Cisco**, the default password for this IOS. (It is case sensitive.) Press **Enter**, and notice that the prompt changes to ap#. This is privileged mode, which is also known as enable mode.

7. Type **show run** and press **Enter**. The current configuration of the access point displays. Press the Spacebar to scroll through the output as necessary. What is the station's role in the network?

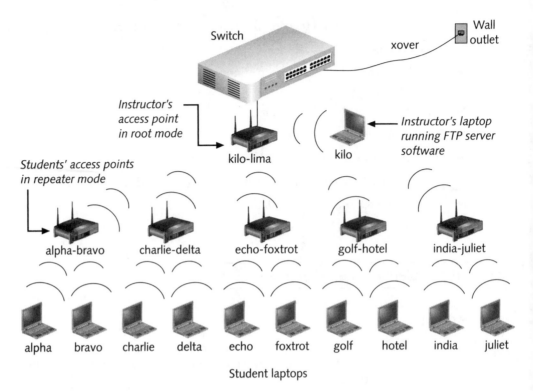

Figure 6-1   Repeater mode lab setup

8. Using the following commands, configure your access point to be a repeater. You may need to press Enter to clear messages.

conf t [Enter]

int dot11radio0 [Enter]

ssid kilo-limawap [Enter]

infrastructure-ssid [Enter]

exit [Enter]

station-role repeater [Enter]

parent 1 [substitute the MAC address for kilo–lima (the instructor's access point) in xxxx.xxxx.xxxx format]

Ctrl+Z

[Enter] (to clear messages)

show run [Enter]

9. Do you see the additional infrastructure SSID kilo-limawap? _____

   This is the SSID your access point will use to associate with the root access point. Do you see station–role repeater? _____

   "Yes" means that your access point is now in repeater mode rather than the default root mode. If your access point is not in repeater mode, you should enter the commands in Step 8 again.

10. Type **show int dot11radio0** and press **Enter**. Your radio interface should be up. If it is not up, ask your instructor for help.

11. Do NOT type "copy run start". You do not want to save the repeater mode configuration, so not issuing the command will ensure that once you unplug your access point, it will return to the previous settings and you will again be able to use it in the more useful root mode.

12. Point to the **ADU** icon in the tray. Your laptop should be connected to your access point in infrastructure mode. You may need to open the Aironet Desktop Utility and activate your Infrastructure Mode profile. Do not continue if you are not connected. What is your connected speed? _____

13. Now you will measure throughput in repeater mode. On your laptop, click **Start**, then click **Run**. Type **cmd** in the text box and press **Enter** to open a DOS window.

14. Type **ftp**, press the Spacebar, and then type the IP address of KILO, which is the instructor laptop now acting as the FTP server. The instructor will give you this IP address. Press **Enter** to open an FTP session with the server.

15. Enter **anonymous** for the username and your e-mail address for the password.

16. Type **dir** to see a listing of files on the FTP server. You should see the tournament.ssf file, which is approximately 77 MB.

17. Type **hash** and press **Enter**. This will allow you to watch the download as a series of hash marks in the DOS window.

18. In the DOS window, type **get tournament.ssf** and press **Enter**. The file should begin downloading.

19. When the download is finished, the throughput in kilobytes per second should be indicated in the DOS window. What is the reported throughput in kilobytes per second? _____

20. To open the Windows calculator, click **Start**, then click **Run**. Type **calc**, then press **Enter**. Convert the throughput in kilobytes per second recorded in Step 19 to megabits per second (Mbps) by multiplying by 8 bits/byte and then dividing by 1000. What is the reported throughput in Mbps?

   _____

21. Calculate the percentage of the rated bandwidth you experienced during the repeater mode download by dividing the reported throughput recorded in Step 20 by the rated bandwidth of your connection. If you are using the 802.11g standard, the rated bandwidth is 54 Mbps.

_____

22. What was the percentage of rated bandwidth, in Mbps, you experienced while transferring the same file in ad hoc mode? This value was recorded in Step 15 of Lab 6.1.

_____

23. What was the percentage of rated bandwidth, in Mbps, you experienced while transferring the same file in basic infrastructure mode? This value was recorded in Step 11 of Lab 6.2. _____

24. What was the percentage of rated bandwidth, in Mbps, you experienced while transferring the same file while roaming? This value was recorded in Step 9 of Lab 5.2.

_____

25. In Table 6.1, enter the file transfer throughputs in Mbps for each of the different labs. If you didn't do Lab 5.2, you will not have a roaming infrastructure entry.

Table 6-1 Throughput Comparison

Configuration	Where Recorded	File Transfer Throughput in Mbps
Ad hoc mode	Lab 6.1, Step 14	
Basic infrastructure mode (BSS)	Lab 6.2, Step 10	
Roaming infrastructure mode (ESS)	Lab 5.2, Step 8	
Repeater mode	Lab 6.3, Step 20	

26. Type **quit** at the ftp prompt in the DOS window, then close the DOS window

27. Open Internet Explorer and browse to your access point using the IP address you recorded in Step 15 of Lab 2.2. Log in as **administrator** with the password **Cisco**. Click **Clients**. Who is associated with your access point?

_____

28. Browse to the access point **kilo-limawap**. The instructor will give you this IP address. Who is associated with this parent access point?

_____

29. Close Internet Explorer.

30. Close HyperTerminal. Save the connection if prompted.

31. Shut down the laptop.

32. Remove the console cable from the laptop and the access point and power down the access point.

Certification Objectives

Objectives for the CWNA exam:

➤ Recognize the concepts associated with wireless LAN service sets

Review Questions

1. Why should you avoid repeater mode if at all possible?

2. What is the purpose of repeater mode?

3. How does repeater mode degrade wireless LAN performance?

4. Approximately what percentage of cell overlap is necessary between the root mode device and the repeater?

5. The repeater itself becomes a client of the root access point. True or False?

LAB 6.4 MEASURING INFRASTRUCTURE MODE THROUGHPUT USING THE LINKSYS WIRELESS ROUTER

Objectives

Many people are using Linksys wireless routers or similar residential wireless gateway devices in their homes or small businesses. These relatively low-cost devices do more networking functions than a basic access point like the Cisco 1200. In addition to accepting wireless clients, many residential wireless gateways also accept wired clients. They also perform network address translation (NAT) and act as routers. While residential wireless gateways are able to handle the wireless traffic of very few users, these devices do not have the configuration options or the power of a device such as the Cisco 1200 series access point. There have been complaints that downloading very large files using residential wireless gateways causes the user's computer to lock up or freeze. In Lab 6.2, you transferred a very large file from one laptop to another through the Cisco 1200 access point. The purpose of this lab is to compare that file transfer throughput to the throughput realized using a residential wireless gateway.

In this lab, you will transfer the same file through a Linksys wireless router that you transferred through the Cisco 1200 series access point. The throughput measured will be compared to the infrastructure mode throughput measured in Lab 6.2.

After completing this lab, you will be able to:

➤ Measure and describe the throughput realized in an infrastructure mode file transfer

➤ Compare the performance of a Linksys wireless router to a Cisco 1200 series access point

Materials Required

This lab requires the following for each team:

➤ Two laptop computers running Windows XP and configured with a Cisco Aironet adapter

➤ One Linksys wireless "G" router

➤ One UTP patch cable

➤ Power cable for the router

➤ 3cs117.zip file (free FTP program provided by instructor)

➤ Tournament.ssf file (file provided by instructor)

➤ Completion of Lab 3.4

➤ Completion of Lab 6.2

Estimated completion time: **35 minutes**

LAB ACTIVITY

ACTIVITY

1. Power up your team's Linksys wireless router. Turn on your team's laptops and log in. Point to the **ADU** icon in the tray. If you are using ad hoc mode instead of infrastructure mode, open the **Aironet Desktop Utility**, click the **Profile Management** tab, and double-click your **Infrastructure Mode** profile to activate it. You should be connected to your wireless router before continuing.

2. On the FTP server laptop, click **Start**, point to **All Programs**, point to **3CServer**, and then click **3CServer**. Make sure the FTP server button is on.

3. You will do the following steps on the FTP client laptop. Click **Start**, then click **Run**. Type **cmd** in the text box and press **Enter** to open a DOS window.

4. Type **ftp** and then follow the command with a **space** and the **IP address** (or name) of the laptop that is serving as the FTP server. Press **Enter** to open an FTP session with the server.

5. Log in as **anonymous** and enter your e-mail address for the password.

6. Type **dir** to see a listing of files on the FTP server. You should see the tournament.ssf file, which is approximately 77 MB.

7. Type **hash** and press **Enter**. This will allow you to watch the download as a series of hash marks in the DOS window.

8. Type **get tournament.ssf** and press **Enter**. The file should begin downloading from the FTP server. If the download hangs before finishing or your laptop locks up, reboot the laptop and attempt to download the file again.

9. When the download is finished, the throughput in kilobytes per second should be indicated in the DOS window. What is the reported throughput in kilobytes per second? _____

10. To open the Windows calculator, click **Start**, then click **Run**. Type **calc**, then press **Enter**. Convert the throughput in kilobytes per second recorded in Step 9 to megabits per second (Mbps) by multiplying by 8 bits/byte and then dividing by 1000. What is the reported throughput in Mbps?

    _____

11. Calculate the percentage of the rated bandwidth you experienced during the download by dividing the reported throughput recorded in Step 10 by the rated bandwidth of your connection. If you are using the 802.11g standard, the rated bandwidth is 54 Mbps. _____

12. What was the file transfer throughput, in Mbps, you experienced while transferring the same file in basic infrastructure mode (BSS)? This value was recorded in Table 6-1 of Lab 6.3. _____

13. Type **quit** at the ftp prompt in the DOS window, then close the DOS window.

14. On the FTP server, close 3CServer.

15. Shut down the laptops.

Certification Objectives

Objectives for the CWNA exam:

➤ Recognize the concepts associated with wireless LAN service sets

Review Questions

1. Describe any interruptions you experienced during the download in the lab activity.

2. How would you describe the performance of the Linksys wireless router as compared to the Cisco 1200 series access point?

3. Theoretically, should there be any performance difference between the Linksys wireless router and the Cisco 1200 series access point? Explain your answer.

4. The Linksys wireless router performs more networking functions than the Cisco 1200. True or False?

5. The Linksys wireless router is more powerful than the Cisco 1200. True or False?

Lab 6.5 Determining if Going Wireless is Worthwhile

Objectives

As an IT professional, you may find yourself in the position of having to justify expanding your network to include wireless devices. Because managers want to see the bottom line, Cisco has come up with ways to calculate how much time, on average, an employee would have to save using the wireless infrastructure to make the investment in wireless worthwhile. Usually, the cost of any new laptops is not included. On the Cisco Web site, you can find the WLAN Productivity Savings Payback Calculator. The purpose of this lab is to become familiar with this tool if you find yourself promoting wireless at your company. Use the following scenario to determine which inputs to use in the program.

Scenario

Your IT Department is preparing a presentation for management focusing on the benefits of extending your network using an 802.11b wireless infrastructure based on the Cisco 1200 series access points. Your company has 800 employees. You don't know how many access points you should deploy, but based on bandwidth calculations, you would not want more than 35 users on an access point at any one time. Your Chief Financial Officer has already said that any new equipment needs to be depreciated in one year. The average yearly salary at your company is $51,000. You estimate that the incremental IT support costs for this infrastructure will be approximately $5,000 per 1000 users. You want to use Cisco's WLAN Productivity Savings Payback Calculator to show management that the new wireless infrastructure will pay for itself very quickly.

After completing this lab, you will be able to:

➤ Use the WLAN Productivity Savings Payback Calculator to calculate how quickly your investment in wireless networking will pay for itself

➤ Understand the variables involved in making the decision to invest in wireless

Materials Required

This lab requires the following for each team:

➤ One laptop computer running Windows XP and configured with a Cisco Aironet adapter

➤ Internet access

Estimated completion time: 20 minutes

ACTIVITY

NOTE

This lab involves the use of a Web site that may have changed since the writing of this lab. Therefore, the exact link names and locations may have changed.

1. If your team will be using the laptops for Internet access, power up your access point and connect it to the classroom switch if necessary. Turn on both laptops and log in.

2. Point to the **ADU** icon in the tray. You should be connected to your access point using the Infrastructure Mode profile. If you are not using the Infrastructure Mode profile, open the **Aironet Desktop Utility** by double-clicking the desktop shortcut. Click the **Profile Management** tab and double-click the **Infrastructure Mode** profile to activate it. In a few seconds, you should connect to your access point.

3. Browse to **www.cisco.com**.

4. Point to **Products and Solutions**.

5. Point to **Wireless**.

6. Click **Aironet 1200 Series Access Point**.

7. Scroll down, if necessary, and click **WLAN Productivity Savings Payback Calculator**.

8. Scroll down, if necessary, and click **Launch the WLAN Productivity Savings Payback Calculator**.

9. Using the scenario above, enter the correct values. You must use the payback calculator to calculate the number of access points needed based on the number of users per access point, as listed in the scenario above. After entering the six variables, click **Next**.

10. How much time must each employee save per day using the wireless infrastructure to pay for the infrastructure and support in one year?

   _____

11. In your opinion, and under these circumstances, would it be relatively easy to convince your boss to implement a wireless infrastructure? _____

   Why or why not?

   _____

Certification Objectives

Lab 6.5 does not map directly to objectives on the exam. However, it teaches a skill that i valuable to wireless networking professionals.

Review Questions

1. How many access points are necessary for your 800 users if you want to limit each access point to 35 associations?

2. According to the payback calculator, what is the WLAN cost per user per day?

3. According to the payback calculator, what is the cost of twenty-two 802.11b access points?

4. According to the payback calculator, what is the cost to do the site survey and install the wireless equipment for this scenario?

5. In your opinion, what are advantages and disadvantages of using the payback calculator when promoting a wireless network at your company?

CONDUCTING A SITE SURVEY

CWNA Exam Objectives	
Objective	**Lab**
Identify and understand the importance and process of conducting a thorough site survey	7.1, 7.2, 7.3
Identify and understand the importance of the necessary tasks to do an RF site survey	7.1, 7.2, 7.3
Identify the necessary equipment needed to perform a site survey	7.1, 7.2, 7.3

Lab 7.1 Using AiroPeek to Analyze a Wireless LAN

Objectives

If you completed Lab 5.5, you installed AiroPeek and used it to capture packets on the wireless network and measure network errors. AiroPeek is a network analyzer for 802.11 networks that can be used to capture traffic, then filter, analyze, and interpret the traffic patterns, data packet contents, statistics, and protocol types. Because of these capabilities, it is often used as a wireless site survey tool. AiroPeek works with all of the latest revisions of the 802.11 standards but doesn't work with all wireless NIC adapters. It also isn't fully compatible with all operating systems. It is very expensive but there is a free demo. The purpose of this lab is to become familiar with the demo version of this product and to evaluate it with wireless site surveying in mind.

In this lab you will download and install AiroPeek and then use it to capture packets on your wireless network. You will then investigate the features of AiroPeek and evaluate it as a site survey tool.

After completing this lab, you will be able to:

➤ Understand the capabilities of AiroPeek

➤ Know how AiroPeek can be used in a wireless site survey

Materials Required

This lab requires the following for each team:

➤ Two laptop computers running Windows XP and configured with a Cisco Aironet adapter

➤ One Cisco Aironet 1200 access point using IOS-based firmware and interface

➤ One UTP patch cable

➤ Power cable for the access point

➤ Access to the wired network through a switch (only one switch is required, regardless of the number of teams)

➤ Completion of the Chapter 2 labs

Estimated completion time: **30 minutes**

ACTIVITY

NOTE

If you did not complete Lab 5.5, you can still do this lab, but you must complete Steps 1 through 27 of Lab 5.5 to download and install AiroPeek first. This lab depends on the WildPackets Web site, which may have changed slightly since the writing of this lab.

1. Power up your team's access point if necessary and connect it to the network switch. Turn on your team's laptops and log in.

2. Point to the **ADU** icon in the tray. You should be connected to your access point using the Infrastructure Mode profile. If you are not connected using the Infrastructure Mode profile, open the **Aironet Desktop Utility** and switch to your Infrastructure Mode profile by double-clicking the profile name.

3. On the non-AiroPeek laptop, open the **Aironet Desktop Utility** on the desktop. What channel are you using? _____

   Close the ADU. You will also need the IP address of your access point, as listed in Table 2-4 of Lab 2.2. What is your access point's IP address? _____

4. On the AiroPeek computer, click **Start**, point to **All Programs**, and then click **WildPackets AiroPeek Demo** to open the program. Read the demo warning and then click **OK**. The AiroPeek laptop is now in promiscuous (sniffing) mode and the adapter is passive. You cannot transmit on this adapter while the AiroPeek program is running. Notice that the ADU icon in the tray is grayed out to indicate your laptop has no connection to the network.

5. On the AiroPeek laptop, click **Monitor**, click **Select Monitor Adapter**, and then click **Cisco Wireless Adapter**, if necessary.

6. Click the **802.11** tab and then click the **Scan** radio button. Click **Edit Scanning Options**. Deselect all channels except the one you recorded in Step 3 and channel 160. You should have two channels selected. Click **OK**, then click **OK** again.

7. Click the **Monitor** menu and make sure the **Monitor Statistics** item is checked. If it is, the demo version will monitor for five minutes. If you try to check the item after it has already monitored for five minutes, you will get an alert message. You will know if you are scanning because you will see movement in the bottom-right pane as you scan the two channels you selected in Step 6.

8. Now you will generate traffic between the non-AiroPeek laptop and your access point. Click **Start** on the non-AiroPeek laptop, then click **Run**. Type **cmd** and press **Enter**. Enter the **ping [ip address]** command but substitute the IP address of your access point, as recorded in Step 3. Next, open Internet Explorer and browse to *www.drudgereport.com*. Open an article to read. Keep

opening links. Eventually, the AiroPeek monitoring will time out. Click **OK** on the AiroPeek laptop when you get the message.

9. To see the results of the monitoring, click the **Monitor** menu, then click **Nodes** in the AiroPeek window. You should see your access point's SSID, and below it, your access point's MAC address. Under that will be the MAC address of your non-AiroPeek laptop. Most likely it will be displayed as Aironet plus the last six digits of the MAC. Aironet identifies Cisco as the OUI (Organizational Unit Identifier) part of the MAC. What channel was your laptop communicating on? _____

10. Double-click the MAC address of your access point. Look in the protocol window. It displays all of the different protocols identified by AiroPeek. Scroll through the display and record the percentages for the following access point packet types.

    Beacons: _____

    HTTP: _____

    DNS: _____

    Echo Request/Echo Reply total: _____

11. Close the Node Statistics window (*not* the AiroPeek program window).

12. Double-click the MAC address of your laptop. Look in the protocol window. Record the percentages for the following laptop packet types.

    HTTP: _____

    DNS: _____

    Echo Request/Echo Reply total: _____

    Probe Request/Probe Response total: _____

13. Close the packet information windows (*not* the AiroPeek program window).

14. On the AiroPeek laptop, click **File**, then click **New**. The Cisco Wireless Adapter should still be selected on the Adapter tab. Click the **Filters** tab and then check **802.11 Beacons** and **HTTP** to select them. Click **OK**. Click **Capture**, then click **Start Capture**.

15. Very quickly, on the non-AiroPeek laptop, begin opening various links on the Drudge Report Web site to generate traffic. The capture will stop after 250 packets or 30 seconds because you are using the demo version. Click **OK**.

16. Click the **Packets** tab at the bottom of the window, if necessary. Scroll through the capture. Scroll to the right and down until you see a beacon frame in the Protocol column. Double-click the line and scroll through the information. Notice that you can see the SSID. This is because the access point is broadcasting the SSID in clear text so client devices using a default profile can connect to it. Close the packet window but don't close the AiroPeek program.

17. Scroll right and down until you see an **HTTP** packet. Double-click it to view the contents. Scroll down and record the following:

    Destination MAC address: _____

    Source MAC address: _____

    Source IP address: _____

    Destination IP address: _____

    Destination port number: _____

    TCP Sequence number: _____

    TCP ACK number: _____

18. Close the packet window. Close the capture window. Don't close AiroPeek.

19. On the non-AiroPeek laptop, return to the command prompt window and type **telnet** followed by the IP address of your access point, as recorded in Step 3. **Don't press Enter yet**.

20. In AiroPeek, click **File** on the menu bar, click **New**, and then click the **Filters** tab. Scroll down and select **Telnet** to limit your capture to Telnet frames. Click **OK**.

21. Click the **Start Capture** button and then quickly press **Enter** on the non-AiroPeek laptop to execute the telnet command. Enter the username **Cisco** and the password **Cisco**. If the capture is still active, enter **enable**, then enter the password **Cisco** to enter enable mode on the access point. Enter the **show run** command.

22. When the capture finishes on the AiroPeek laptop, scroll to the far right until you see the **Summary** column. Scroll down and look at the text that is in black. This text represents the words that displayed on the non-AiroPeek laptop during the Telnet login. You should be able to see the Cisco password as well as any other text that appeared in the Telnet window. Most of the password information is sent one character at a time and appears as a column of single characters.

23. Notice the tabs across the bottom of the top frame. Click the tabs, one by one, to see the various views of the captured packets.

24. Close any open windows. Shut down the laptops.

Certification Objectives

Objectives for the CWNA exam:

➤ Identify and understand the importance and process of conducting a thorough site survey

➤ Identify and understand the importance of the necessary tasks to do an RF site survey

➤ Identify the necessary equipment needed to perform a site survey

Review Questions

1. What value is there in observing the different protocol types and their percentages in a packet capture?

2. Why were you able to see the SSID in the capture?

3. Telnet is a secure method of configuring your access point. True or False?

4. How could the information obtained in Step 17 be used in an attack?

5. What is your opinion of AiroPeek as a tool for monitoring wireless networks?

LAB 7.2 USING AIRMAGNET TO EVALUATE THE PERFORMANCE AND SECURITY OF A WIRELESS LAN

Objectives

AirMagnet is another wireless sniffer tool that provides WLAN management and security software systems for handheld, laptop, and network configurations. Like many wireless analyzers, AirMagnet helps solve wireless connection problems, tracks down unauthorized access, finds rogue access points, and simplifies site surveys. Unlike traditional packet scanners and protocol analyzers such as AiroPeek that have been adapted from their original purpose to analyze wired networks, AirMagnet was designed specifically for wireless LANs. AirMagnet displays a high-quality graphical user interface, which provides an overall view of the network on a single screen. The tool detects problems using a range of alerts, and can troubleshoot security and performance issues, in some cases providing solutions to the problems. This software can even help you enforce your security policy. Like AiroPeek, AirMagnet is very expensive, but there is a demo version. The demo provides for a seven-minute capture, and once installed, stops working after seven days. The purpose of this lab is to investigate the demo version of AirMagnet.

In this lab, you will use AirMagnet to capture and analyze traffic generated on the wireless LAN. You will investigate the features of AirMagnet and evaluate it as a wireless site survey tool.

After completing this lab, you will be able to:

➤ Understand the capabilities of AirMagnet

➤ Understand how AirMagnet can be used to evaluate security and performance on your wireless LAN

Materials Required

This lab requires the following for each team:

➤ Two laptop computers running Windows XP and configured with a Cisco Aironet adapter

➤ One Cisco Aironet 1200 access point using IOS-based firmware and interface

➤ One UTP patch cable

➤ Power cable for the access point

➤ Access to the wired network through a switch (only one switch is required, regardless of the number of teams)

➤ Completion of the Chapter 2 labs

Estimated completion time: **60 minutes**

ACTIVITY

This lab depends on AirMagnet's Web site, which may have changed slightly since the writing of this lab.

NOTE

1. Connect and power up your team's access point if necessary. Turn on your team's laptops and log in. Point to the **ADU** icon in the tray. You should be connected to your access point using the Infrastructure Mode profile before continuing. If necessary, open the **Aironet Desktop Utility** from the desktop and activate the Infrastructure Mode profile.

2. You will download and install AirMagnet on the laptop that is *not* configured with AiroPeek. If you have not installed AiroPeek, it doesn't matter which laptop you configure AirMagnet on. Open **Internet Explorer** and browse to *www.airmagnet.com*. Click **Products**, then click **Laptop Analyzer**.

3. Click **Demo** and fill in the registration form. Select **Laptop Analyzer**, then select any referral source and click **Submit**.

4. Click **Laptop 5-minute demo**, then click **Download Laptop Demo** and save it to your desktop.

5. Close all windows and double-click the downloaded file to begin installation. Accept all default settings during the installation until you are prompted for the adapter.

6. When prompted for the adapter, click **Cisco Systems**. Click the **802.11a/b/g card** if necessary. Click **Next**. Click **Continue Anyway** when you get the hardware installation warning and then click **Finish**.

7. Click **Start**, point to **All Programs**, point to **AirMagnet**, and click **Demo**. Click **OK** when the Days Left to Evaluate window displays. When AirMagnet launches, it immediately begins capturing packets in Live Capture mode. The demo version provides for a seven-minute capture. When a window informs you that the capture has stopped, you must close the AirMagnet program and restart it to begin live capturing again. Remember that your adapter will be unavailable while AirMagnet is capturing packets. This is true of almost all adapters when they are in promiscuous mode (sniffing).

8. While the AirMagnet laptop is capturing packets, you should surf the Web, ping Web sites, and telnet to your access point to generate traffic from the non-AirMagnet laptop.

9. Maximize the AirMagnet window to see the complete display, as shown in Figure 7-1. In the upper-left corner is the RF signal level meter, which provides an overview of the signal quality on all channels. By default, AirMagnet opens an RF signal meter window for both 802.11a and 802.11b/g networks.

10. The RF signal meter window displays a bar for each channel. If you completed Lab 7.1, you recorded your equipment's channel in Step 3 of that lab. What channel is your team's equipment laptop using? _____

   (*Hint:* Use the ADU program to determine the channel if you did not do Lab 7.1.)

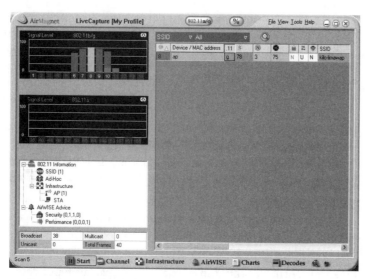

Figure 7-1   AirMagnet

11. The channel bars are color-coded. Green means that access points or stations are operating on that channel. This could be used to find a rogue access point operating on a channel you know should not be configured for use on your network. Red indicates noise. Cordless phones, Web cameras, and microwave ovens can cause interference with 2.4-GHz signals. Red levels above 10 percent or 75 dBm can result in high packet error rates and poor network performance. What is the percentage of red on your channel? _____

Click the **percentage sign** on the title bar to switch to dBm view. What is the approximate dBm of the red on your channel? _____

Brown denotes cross-channel interference. Because your lab environment may have exceeded the maximum number of DSSS access points in a single coverage area, you may see a lot of brown as the channels are overlapping and interfering with each other.

12. Expand the channel view by clicking the **down arrow** in the upper-right corner of the signal level window. This expanded view displays signal level, noise level, and signal-to-noise ratio (SNR) in separate graphs. The down arrow changes to an up arrow when you expand the view. Click the **up arrow** to return to the collapsed view of the signal level.

13. After seven minutes, the AirMagnet demo will cease capturing packets and display a notification window. Click **OK** when this window displays, then close and reopen AirMagnet to begin another seven-minute capture.

14. The 802.11 Information window on the left of your screen is a summary of your WLAN infrastructure. It categorizes all the devices detected on your wireless network and shows the total number of devices in each category. Access points are listed as AP and laptops are listed as STA. The laptops running AirMagnet are not included in the list because they are in promiscuous mode and are not transmitting. Also in the 802.11 Information window is a section named "AirWISE advice." This section displays alarms for security and performance. There are four sets of digits for each category, which represent different levels of severity. The digits from left to right represent the following status: Critical, Urgent, Warning, and Informational. Look at the Security category. How many urgent security matters has AirMagnet found on this wireless LAN? _____

15. Double-click the **Performance** alarm to jump to the AirWISE screen. You will investigate AirWISE in more detail later in the lab. Click the **Start** button at the bottom of the screen to return to the original display.

16. In the lower-left corner of the display is a table of packet types detected on your wireless network. The packets are categorized as broadcast, unicast, and multicast. What is the most prevalent type of packet on your wireless LAN?

   _____

17. On the right side of the window is the RF Data Summary table, which categorizes the data 16 ways. You can sort the table by any category by clicking the header of that column. Click the **SSID** column header to sort by that category and find your SSID. Scroll to the right to view all of the data for your SSID. You can sort the data by SSID or channel using the filters in the upper-left corner of the table. Click **SSID** in the upper-left corner, then click **Channel**. Are any other SSIDs using your same channel? _____

   If yes, which one(s)?

   _____

18. The column with the red lock in the row header refers to the security mechanism being used by the device. "N" means WEP disabled, "Y" means WEP required, "V" means PPTP, IPSec, SSH, and other encrypted systems other than WEP are in use, and "1x" means 802.1x is in use. What is the designation for your SSID? _____

   Is your equipment using any encryption? _____

19. Look in the lower-left corner of the AirMagnet window. If AirMagnet has stopped scanning, close the program and reopen it to begin a new seven-minute scan.

20. Walk your AirMagnet laptop out of the room and around the building. Watch the green channel bar for your channel. The green area should decrease as you move away from your access point. Are you able to detect any new access points? _____

If so, is encryption being used on these access points? _____

If yes, what type of encryption is being used? _____

Walk your laptop back to class.

21. Notice that some fields in the RF Data Summary table are also color-coded. In this case, red on a channel indicates that an alarm is set on that channel, red on Device/MAC address means the device has been inactive for at least 60 seconds, yellow on Device/MAC address means the device has been inactive between 5 and 60 seconds, green on Device/MAC address indicates the device has been inactive in the last five seconds, and gray on Device/MAC address means the device is inactive (down). What is the color of your channel field? _____

What is the color of your Device/MAC address field? _____

22. Look in the lower-left corner of the AirMagnet window. If AirMagnet has stopped scanning, close the program and reopen it to begin a new seven-minute scan. Generate some traffic on the non-AirMagnet laptop by surfing the Web, pinging the access point, and telnetting to the access point. On the AirMagnet laptop, click the **Channel** button at the bottom of the screen. Click your channel from among the line of channels along the top of the screen. In the top left, the window displays channel utilization. In the top right, the window displays throughput. What is your channel's approximate bandwidth utilization? _____

What is your channel's approximate throughput? _____

As a rule of thumb, 60 percent utilization, which translates to 30 Mbps through-put on an 802.11a or 802.11b network, is a realistic upper limit for 802.11g networks. Do your numbers fall within this range? _____

If your numbers are outside the rule of thumb, what could explain this problem? _____

23. Make sure you are still scanning. Click the **Infrastructure** button at the bottom of the screen to switch to Infrastructure view. This view shows a lot of the same parameters as Channel view, but the focus is on devices rather than channels. Expand your **SSID** in the left pane by clicking the plus sign, then click your access point's **MAC address** or **name**. Information displayed includes speed, media type, alert frames, control frames, management frames, data frames, and access point details. Click **Speed** if necessary to expand the display. Notice that the number of transmit and receive frames are listed for each speed designation.

24. Click the **AirWISE** button at the bottom of the screen. AirWISE is the engine that provides the alarm feature in AirMagnet. Expand the **Performance** category, if necessary, by clicking the plus sign beside it. The numbers in parentheses indicate the total number of alarms detected in that category. (See Figure 7-2.)

7

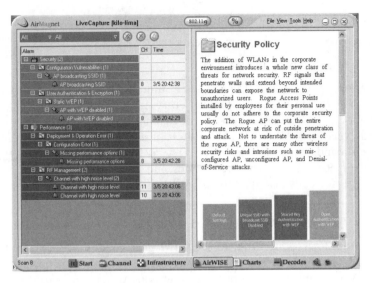

Figure 7-2 AirWISE

25. The left side of the screen displays alarms, which are arranged as a hierarchy of network policies. You can switch from Alarm Tree view to Alarm List view. Click the button with the triangle on it at the top of the window. The Alarm List view displays. This screen allows you to sort the alarms by channel, alarm, time, or source. You do that by clicking the column header. You may need to drag the column borders to see all four columns, which include channel, alarm, time, and source node. Click the **CH** column header to sort by channel. Click the **plus sign** button to switch back to the Alarm Tree view.

26. Look in the **Time** column. Notice that color-coding is used for easy reading and interpretation. Red means critical, orange means urgent, yellow means warning, and blue means informational. List the color and status indicated for the following alarms listed in Table 7-1. Some of these alarms may not be displayed for your system.

Table 7-1 AirMagnet alarms

Alarm	Color	Status
AP broadcasting SSID		
AP with WEP disabled		
Missing performance options		

27. If it is present, click the **AP broadcasting SSID** alarm row for your channel and look at the right side of the screen, which is the Expert Advice pane. Summarize the information you are given by AirWISE.

_____

_____

28. If it is present, click the **AP with WEP disabled** alarm row for your channel and look at the right side of the screen, which is the Expert Advice pane. Summarize the information you are given by AirWISE.

_____

_____

29. Make sure AirMagnet is still scanning. If it is not scanning, close the AirMagnet program and reopen it to begin a new seven-minute scan.

30. Click the **Charts** button at the bottom of the screen. This screen allows you to identify the "top 10" to be charted. The top 10 can be access points, stations, nodes, or channels. You can further define the top 10 by filtering on speed, frame type, address, or media. Choose the **top 10 channels** by clicking the associated list box. Filter on **802.11 frame type** by clicking the associated list box. Based on the table below the chart, record the following percentages for your channel in Table 7-2.

Table 7-2   Percentage of 802.11 frame types

802.11 Frame Type	Percentage
Control frames	
Management frames	
Data frames	
CRC frames	

31. Click the **Graph Options** button, which is at the top of the Charts screen. Select your channel and change to 2D view. Click **OK**. Next, use the list boxes to choose the **top 10 APs** and filter on **frame speed**. What speed are the majority of the frames experiencing using your channel?

_____

32. The last thing you will do in this lab is create a capture filter. Click the **Decodes** button at the bottom of the screen. Change the channel to your channel if necessary using the list box. Click the **File** menu, then click **Configure**. Configure the capture as specified in Table 7-3, then click **OK** when you finish.

Table 7-3   Capture filter parameters

Tab	Change
Profile	Type your team name (not SSID), then click New and switch to your team name using the list box
General	Make sure "New AP discovered" is selected, then choose a sound from the list of choices
802.11	Change the SSID to yours (for example, Charlie-deltawap)
Filter	Make sure Control and Data frames are selected and Management frames are not selected

33. Notice that your new filter profile name, which is your team name, displays on the title bar. If AirMagnet is not scanning, close AirMagnet, then reopen it to initiate a new live capture. (See Figure 7-3.) Maximize the window.

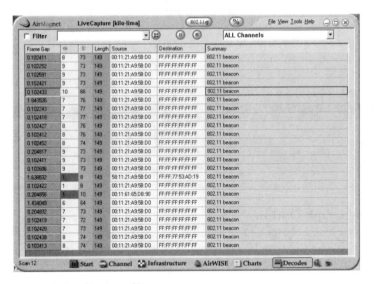

Figure 7-3   Capture filter

34. Begin generating traffic on the non-AirMagnet laptop as before. On the AirMagnet laptop, click **Decodes** at the bottom of your screen if necessary, and watch as the live capture picks up and displays the packets based on your new filter profile.

35. Close any open windows and shut down the laptops.

Certification Objectives

Objectives for the CWNA exam:

➤ Identify and understand the importance and process of conducting a thorough site survey

➤ Identify and understand the importance of the necessary tasks to do an RF site survey

➤ Identify the necessary equipment needed to perform a site survey

Review Questions

7

1. What does red indicate in the RF signal level meter?

2. What is the purpose of the AirWISE section of AirMagnet?

3. How does knowing the different speeds at which data packets are transmitted and received help a network administrator?

4. What feature does AirMagnet have that AiroPeek does not have?

5. What is your opinion of AirMagnet as a tool for monitoring wireless networks?

Lab 7.3 Using Network Stumbler to Find Access Points and Monitor Signal-to-Noise Ratio (SNR)

Objectives

Network Stumbler is probably the most widely used wireless site survey tool. It allows you to detect wireless networks using 802.11a, 802.11b, and 802.11g, and can verify your network parameters, find RF shadows, detect interference, detect rogue access points, and help fine-tune antenna position. Network Stumbler doesn't work with all wireless NIC adapters. It also isn't fully compatible with all operating systems. But unlike AiroPeek and

AirMagnet, it doesn't require special drivers, you can transmit and receive while using it, and it is free. The purpose of this lab is to become familiar with this very popular Windows-based product.

In this lab you will install and configure Network Stumbler, then use it to evaluate your wireless environment.

After completing this lab, you will be able to:

➤ Understand the capabilities of Network Stumbler

➤ Understand how Network Stumbler can be used as a wireless site survey tool

Materials Required

This lab requires the following for each team:

➤ Two laptop computers running Windows XP and configured with a Cisco Aironet adapter

➤ One Linksys Wireless "G" router or one Cisco 1200 series access point

➤ One UTP patch cable

➤ Power cable for the router or access point

➤ Access to the wired network through a switch (only one switch is required, regardless of the number of teams)

➤ Completion of the Chapter 2 labs

Estimated completion time: **20 minutes**

ACTIVITY

NOTE

This lab depends on the NetStumbler Web site, which may have changed slightly since the writing of this lab. If you have already installed Network Stumbler in a previous activity, skip to Step 4.

1. Connect and power up your team's Linksys wireless G router or Cisco 1200 access point. If you are using the Linksys router, make sure you connect your router to the switch using the Internet port on the router. Turn on both of your laptops and log in. Use your **Infrastructure Mode** profile. Your laptops should be connected to your wireless router or access point using the Infrastructure Mode profile before continuing.

2. You will download and install Network Stumbler on the non-AiroPeek laptop. If you did not do the AiroPeek labs, you can download and install Network Stumbler on either laptop. On the non-AiroPeek laptop, open Internet Explorer and browse to *www.netstumbler.com*. Click **Downloads** and then click **NetStumbler 0.4.0 Installer**. Save the file to the desktop.

3. Close all windows and double-click the downloaded file to begin installation. Accept all default settings.

4. Close the Help screen if it opens. Double-click the **Network Stumbler** short-cut on the desktop to open the program. Maximize both windows if necessary. Make sure the other laptop is on and connected to your access point.

5. In the Network Stumbler window, expand **Channels** on the left by clicking the plus sign next to it. Which channels are being used?

   _____

6. Expand **Filters** by clicking the plus sign beside it. Click **Encryption On**. Does anything display in the right pane? _____

   Why or why not?

   _____

7. Click **ESS (AP)**. What displays in the right pane of the window?

   _____

8. Click **IBSS (Peer)**. What displays in the right pane of the window?

   _____

   Can you explain the difference between an ESS and an IBSS?

   _____

9. Click **Default SSID**. What displays in the right pane?

   _____

   What is the default SSID for Cisco products?

   _____

   (*Hint:* See Lab 2.2 if you don't remember.)

10. Click **SSIDs**. Right-click the MAC address of your access point in the right pane. Click to look up the address at ARIN, which is the regional registry for IP addresses. What valuable information displays?

    _____

    Notice that unlike AiroPeek and AirMagnet, which are true wireless analyzers, Network Stumbler allows you to transmit on your adapter while using the program.

11. Close the Internet Explorer window with the lookup information.

12. Expand **SSIDs** by clicking the plus sign next to it. Click the **plus** sign next to your SSID to expand it if necessary. If there is no plus sign next to your SSID, click the **plus** sign next to your channel number. Click the MAC address displayed below your SSID or channel number. A graph of signal-to-noise ratio (SNR) versus time should display in the right pane. If RSSI displays instead of SNR in dBm, click the **Device** menu and then click the other adapter listed to select it. Scroll to the right to see the latest data, and real-time graphing. According to Network Stumbler, the red area represents noise, the green area represents good signal, and purple represents no signal. (See Figure 7-4.)

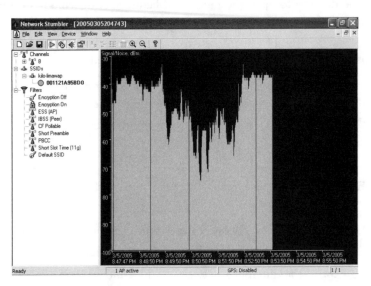

Figure 7-4   Network Stumbler SNR graph

13. Point to the ADU icon in the tray. What is your connected bandwidth?

_____

Take this lab manual and the Network Stumbler laptop and walk away from your access point or wireless router. Continue walking while watching the red area of the graph. What is happening to the red area and why?

_____

What is happening to the green area and why?

_____

Continue to walk away from your access point until you are dissociated with it.

14. While you are walking around the building, you may pick up one or more additional access points. Network Stumbler makes a sound when it finds a new access point. If you find a new access point, click its SSID in the left pane to display information about it in the right pane. Scroll to the right and look in the Encryption column. If encryption is associated with an access point, a lock displays in the Encryption column. Is encryption associated with any of the access points that Network Stumbler has found? _____

   If yes, what type of encryption is it?

   _____

15. Begin walking back to the classroom. Continue to walk slowly while watching the ADU icon in the tray. Stop if the icon turns yellow or red and point to it. Your laptop may have jumped to a designated bandwidth for your particular radio specification. The bandwidth jumps are in increments particular to the 802.11 standard you are using. For example, a B radio will only operate at 1, 2, 5.5, or 11 Mbps. It will never operate at 8 Mbps. G radios only operate at 1, 2, 5.5, 6, 9, 11, 12, 18, 24, 36, 48, and 54 Mbps. Return to the classroom. At this point your laptop should be reassociated with your access point and connected at the maximum bandwidth for your radio connection.

16. Close any open windows. Don't save if prompted. Shut down the laptops.

Certification Objectives

Objectives for the CWNA exam:

➤ Identify and understand the importance and process of conducting a thorough site survey

➤ Identify and understand the importance of the necessary tasks to do an RF site survey

➤ Identify the necessary equipment needed to perform a site survey

Review Questions

1. What bandwidth designations do 802.11b and 802.11g radios have in common?

2. What is the relationship between signal-to-noise ratio and distance?

3. Network Stumbler can find rogue access points. True or False?

4. List some reasons why Network Stumbler is so widely used.

5. What is your opinion of Network Stumbler as a tool for monitoring wireless networks?

WIRELESS LAN SECURITY AND VULNERABILITIES

Labs included in this chapter

➤ Lab 8.1 Creating and Applying a MAC Filter

➤ Lab 8.2 Configuring Open Authentication with WEP

➤ Lab 8.3 Using SSIDs in a More Secure Manner

➤ Lab 8.4 Spoofing a MAC Address

CWNA Exam Objectives	
Objective	Lab
Identify the strengths, weaknesses, and appropriate uses of wireless LAN security techniques	8.1, 8.2, 8.4
Describe the types of wireless LAN security attacks, and explain how to identify and prevent them	8.3, 8.4

LAB 8.1 CREATING AND APPLYING A MAC FILTER

Objectives

One of the simplest ways to add security to your wireless LAN is by implementing filters that almost all wireless access points and wireless routers support. Filters deny or permit traffic through the ports on the wireless infrastructure device. Filters are also known as access lists. You can set up individual filters or sets of filters. You can filter on protocol, IP address, and MAC address. MAC address filters permit or deny the forwarding of unicast and multicast packets either sent from or addressed to specific MAC addresses. Just like access lists on a router, deploying filters is a two-step process. First you create the filter, and then it must be applied to an inbound or outbound interface. In the case of filters on access points, you will usually apply the filters to the radio interface or the Ethernet interface. MAC filtering is not very secure because MAC addresses can be sniffed easily, even when encryption is in use. Once the MAC addresses are known, an intruder can configure his client device to spoof one of these addresses and defeat the filter. Still, MAC address filtering is better than nothing, and is often used on SOHO networks to prevent casual drive-by surfers from stealing bandwidth. The purpose of this lab is to learn how to create and apply MAC filters.

In this lab, you will create and apply a MAC address filter that will block one of your laptops from communicating on the network. You will test the filter, then delete it and test it again to make sure you can communicate.

After completing this lab, you will be able to:

➤ Understand how to create and apply a MAC filter

➤ Understand the limitations of MAC filtering as a wireless security solution

Materials Required

This lab requires the following for each team:

➤ Two laptop computers running Windows XP and configured with a Cisco Aironet adapter

➤ One Cisco Aironet 1200 access point using IOS-based firmware and interface

➤ One UTP patch cable

➤ Power cable for the access point

➤ Access to the wired network through a switch

➤ Completion of the Chapter 2 labs

Estimated completion time: **20 minutes**

ACTIVITY

1. Connect and power up your access point if necessary. Turn on your laptops. Make sure your laptops are using the **Infrastructure Mode** profile.

2. On one laptop, browse to your access point using Internet Explorer. You will need the IP address of your access point. The IP addresses are listed in Table 2-4 in Lab 2.2. The username is **administrator**. The password is **Cisco**. What is the IP address of your access point? _____

3. Click **Association**. Record the MAC address of the laptop you are using to browse the access point. _____

4. Click **Services** in the left pane. Click **Filters**, then click the **MAC Address Filters** tab.

5. Make sure **<NEW>** is selected in the Create/Edit Filter Index menu. In the Filter Index field, enter **700**. Just like access lists on a router, specific number ranges are used depending on the filter type.

6. In the Add MAC Address field, enter the MAC address of the laptop you are using to configure the access point. You recorded this MAC address in Step 3. Enter the address with periods separating the three groups of four characters (for example, 0040.9673.adb0), and make sure you use all lowercase letters, even though uppercase appears to be indicated.

7. Make sure there are all "0"s in the Mask entry field. This is not a subnet mask; it is called a wildcard mask or an inverse mask. It is used with access lists to indicate which bits in the filtered address are significant. Zeroes are significant, but ones are not. All "0"s will force the access point to match every bit of the MAC address. This means any MAC address being filtered must be an exact match of the one you have entered.

8. Select **Forward** from the Action menu, if necessary. Make sure the default action is **Block All** so only the MAC address you configured will be permitted, then click **Add**. The filter should appear in the Filters Classes field.

9. Click **Apply**, then click **OK** in the warning window. Filter 700 has been created but not applied to an interface. Until the next steps are completed, your filter is not filtering.

10. Click the **Apply Filters** tab to return to the Apply Filters page.

11. At the intersection of the incoming row and the Radio0-802.11 column, use the MAC list box to apply MAC filter 700 inbound on the radio interface. This configuration means that only traffic with the configured MAC address can get in to the network via the radio port on your access point. Click **Apply**, then click **OK** to complete the two-step filter process.

12. On the other laptop, navigate to the command prompt window and **ping** the access point, as recorded in Step 2. What was the ping response?
_____

8

Does your filter appear to be working? _____

You should *not* have been able to ping, but if your ping was successful, return to the Internet browser interface on the first laptop, click **System Software**, click **System Configuration**, and then click **Restart** to restart the access point. Once the access point reloads, pinging from the blocked laptop should be unsuccessful.

13. If necessary, log back in to the access point via Internet Explorer. Click **Association**. You may see the blocked laptop in the Association table, even though that laptop cannot send data through the access point. Client devices can remain in the Association table as unauthenticated clients. Does your blocked client device still appear in the Association table? _____

14. Now you must remove the filter. Click **Services**, click **Filters**, and then click the **Apply Filters** tab, if necessary. Change the 700 entry back to **<NONE>** in the list box, click **Apply**, and then click **OK**. You have not removed the filter from the access point, but you have removed the application of the filter, so it has ceased filtering.

15. Click the **MAC Address Filters** tab. Make sure that **700** appears in the Create/Edit Filter Index list box. Click the **Delete** button (not the Delete Class button) at the bottom of the screen, then click **OK** to delete the filter completely. It should no longer be in the Create/Edit Filter Index list box.

16. On the other laptop, navigate to the command prompt window and ping the access point again. What was the ping response? _____

Your ping should have been successful. If it wasn't, make sure you have removed the application of the filter and then the filter, in that order.

17. Close all windows and shut down the laptops.

Certification Objectives

Objectives for the CWNA exam:

➤ Identify the strengths, weaknesses, and appropriate uses of wireless LAN security techniques

Review Questions

1. What is another name for filters?

2. What are the two steps required to deploy filters?

3. How can MAC address filters be defeated by hackers?

4. What is a wildcard or inverse mask and how is it used with access lists?

5. Client devices that are blocked from communicating on the network may still appear in an access point's Association table. True or False?

LAB 8.2 CONFIGURING OPEN AUTHENTICATION WITH WEP

8

Objectives

The 802.11 standards specify two methods of authentication—open and shared-key. Open authentication is the default setting on Cisco devices and is considered "null authentication" because no authentication is really involved. Using open authentication, any device with the same SSID as the access point can authenticate and associate to it. You can make open authentication more secure by configuring it to use wired equivalent privacy (WEP). When WEP is in use, any wireless device can communicate with an access point, but only if its preconfigured WEP keys match. Devices that are not using WEP may authenticate and associate with an access point that is using WEP, but they will not be able to send data. WEP is relatively easy to configure and does not require additional components such as a RADIUS server. Open authentication with WEP encrypts the data after authentication and association have been completed. Layer 1 and 2 information, including beacons, is not encrypted by WEP, but information at layer 3 and higher, including IP addresses, is encrypted. The purpose of this lab is to become familiar with open authentication with WEP by configuring it on the access point and then creating profiles on the clients so they can communicate with the access point in this mode. You will also see the effects of static WEP on a live capture using AiroPeek.

In this lab, you will configure open authentication with WEP on your access point. You will then create a new profile on your laptops using the same WEP key you configured on the access point. Next you will capture and analyze packets using the AiroPeek program. Finally, you will remove the open authentication with WEP configuration from the access point and reassociate with the access point using the Infrastructure Mode profile.

After completing this lab, you will be able to:

➤ Configure open authentication with WEP on the access point

➤ Configure a client profile for open authentication with WEP

➤ Explain what can and can't be seen in a packet capture when WEP is in use

Materials Required

This lab requires the following for each team:

➤ Two laptop computers running Windows XP and configured with a Cisco Aironet adapter

➤ One Cisco Aironet 1200 access point using IOS-based firmware and interface

➤ One UTP patch cable

➤ Power cable for the access point

➤ Access to the wired network through a switch (only one switch is required, regardless of the number of teams)

➤ Completion of the Chapter 2 labs

Estimated completion time: **45 minutes**

LAB ACTIVITY

ACTIVITY

NOTE

This lab assumes that you have completed Lab 5.5, which installed a program called AiroPeek. If you did not complete Lab 5.5, you can still do this lab, but you must complete Steps 1 through 27 of Lab 5.5 to download and install AiroPeek first.

1. Connect and power up your team's access point if necessary. Turn on both of your laptops and log in. Use the **Infrastructure Mode** profile.

2. On the laptop you used to download AiroPeek, browse to your access point using the IP address you configured in Lab 2.2 and recorded in Step 2 of Lab 8.1.

3. Click **Security** and review the Security Summary table. Notice that open authentication is being used with no additional security features. There is no data encryption or server-based authentication. The access point is wide open.

4. Click **Encryption Manager**. Select **Cipher** and make sure **WEP 128 bit** (not TKIP + WEP 128 bit) is selected.

5. Click **Transmit Key** for **Encryption Key 1** and type **123456789** for the encryption key. **128 bit** should be selected as the key size.

6. Scroll down and click **Apply**. You will see an error window. What is the problem? _____

   Click **OK** to close the error window.

7. Scroll back up and change your cipher to **WEP 40 bit** strength. Change the key size for the encryption to **40 bit**. Click **Apply**. How many hexadecimal characters does 40-bit encryption require? _____

   Click **OK**.

8. Change the key to **0123456789** and click **Apply**. Click **OK**. You will lose your connection to the access point. Why?

   _____

9. On both laptops, open the **Aironet Desktop Utility** from the shortcut on the desktop. Create a new profile named **Open Authentication with WEP**. Configure your SSID name (for example, golf-hotelwap) in the **SSID1** text box. On the **Security** tab, select **Pre-Shared Key (static WEP)** and then click the **Configure** button.

10. Click in the **WEP key 1** text box and enter **0123456789**. Make sure **Hexadecimal (0-9, A-F)** and a key size of **40** are selected. Click **OK**, then click **OK** again to return to the Profile Management window.

11. Double-click the **Open Authentication with WEP** profile to activate it. Within a few seconds, you should be reconnected. Click the **Current Status** tab. What channel is your equipment using? _____

    Close the Aironet Desktop Utility.

12. On the AiroPeek laptop, click **Start**, point to **All Programs**, and then click **WildPackets AiroPeek Demo** to open the program. Click **OK**. You will lose your connectivity while AiroPeek is open.

13. Click **File** and then click **New** to begin the creation of a new capture.

14. Click the **802.11** tab, and change the Number field to reflect the channel you recorded in Step 11.

15. Click the **Filters** tab, and then select **802.11 Beacons**, **802.11 WEP Packets**, and **Telnet**. Click **OK**.

16. On the non-AiroPeek laptop, open the command prompt window and type **telnet [ip address of access point]**, substituting your access point's IP address where indicated. Do not press Enter yet.

17. In AiroPeek, click the **Start Capture** button and then, very quickly on the non-AiroPeek laptop, press **Enter** to telnet to your access point. The username is **Cisco**. The password is **Cisco**. If you get to the ap> prompt, press **Enter**, then enter **enable** to access privileged exec mode. When prompted for a password, enter **Cisco**. Enter the **show run** command and scroll through the display using the Spacebar.

18. Very soon, the AiroPeek capture will end. Click **OK**. Also, the Monitor Statistics function will end at some point. When you see the notification window, click **OK** and continue with the lab.

8

19. In AiroPeek, scroll to the right in the capture window. Scroll down. In the protocol column, you should see beacons and WEP data, but no Telnet packets. Why not?

_____

20. Double-click a beacon row. Scroll through the top window. Notice that the header information is still viewable in clear text. You should be able to see the name of the access point (ap), the SSID, and the source and destination MAC addresses. Why are you able to see this information, even though WEP encryption is in use?

_____

Look for IP addresses. Do you see any? _____

Why or why not?

_____

Close the packet window but not the capture window.

21. Double-click a WEP data row. Notice that the status field in the Packet Information section indicates encryption is being used. Scroll down until you see the WEP data section. Notice that the WEP initialization vector (IV) is shown. Because static WEP IVs repeat, this information can be used by hackers to crack WEP keys. Close the packet window and then close the capture window, but do not close AiroPeek.

22. Click **File** and then click **New** to create another capture. On the **Filters** tab, select only **ICMP**. Click **OK**.

23. On the non-AiroPeek laptop, return to the command prompt window and enter the **quit** command to end the Telnet session. Type **ping [ip address of access point]**, substituting the IP address of your access point. Do not press Enter yet.

24. In AiroPeek, click the **Start Capture** button and then, very quickly on the non-AiroPeek laptop, press **Enter** to ping your access point. Press the **up arrow** to retrieve the ping command and press **Enter** again. Notice that no packets are being captured. If WEP data packets had been selected in the filter, you would have captured the ICMP packets as WEP data packets.

25. Eventually, the AiroPeek capture will end. Click **OK**. Close the AiroPeek program, then restart the laptop and log on. The restart is usually necessary to reconnect to the access point after using AiroPeek.

26. On the non-AiroPeek laptop, telnet to your access point. The username is **Cisco** and the password is **Cisco**. Enter **en** at the ap> prompt to switch to enable mode. Enter the secret password **Cisco**.

27. Enter the **show run** command to see your access point's new configuration as it displays in the Cisco IOS. Press the Spacebar to scroll down until you see the two new encryption commands:

    Encryption key 1 size 40bit

    Encryption mode ciphers wep40

    These commands resulted from your configuration via the Web browser. Next you will use the "no" form of one of the commands listed above to erase WEP from the access point configuration. Enter the following commands:

    conf t [Enter]

    int dot11radio0 [Enter]

    no encryption mode ciphers wep40 [Enter]

28. Your laptops will lose their connections. Why?

    _____

    On both laptops, open the **Aironet Desktop Utility** from the desktop shortcut.

29. Click the **Profile Management** tab if necessary and double-click the **Infrastructure Mode** profile to activate it. The laptops should reassociate with your access point.

30. Close all windows and shut down the laptops.

Certification Objectives

Objectives for the CWNA exam:

➤ Identify the strengths, weaknesses, and appropriate uses of wireless LAN security techniques

Review Questions

1. Non-WEP clients may be able to associate with WEP devices. True or False?

2. Beacons and MAC addresses can be seen even if WEP encryption is in use. True or False?

3. Which layers of the OSI model are encrypted when WEP is in use?

4. Why is WEP's initialization vector (IV) considered a security weakness?

5. List the two ways you accessed your access point for configuration in this lab. How do you configure an access point if you lose network connectivity?

LAB 8.3 USING SSIDS IN A MORE SECURE MANNER

Objectives

SSIDs are also known as network names and operate like workgroups by subdividing the wireless network. By default the SSID tsunami is configured on most Cisco access points as a guest mode SSID. When an SSID operates in guest mode, it is broadcast in beacons at the prescribed beacon interval. Guest mode means that anyone with a wireless client can hear the SSID and automatically associate with the access point that is advertising it. In Lab 2.1, you configured your access point to use a different SSID than tsunami. However, the new SSID is still being broadcast by your access point in beacons, as it is a guest mode SSID. You can disable guest mode on the Cisco 1200 series access point. When you do this, the SSID will not be broadcast in beacons; rather, the client laptops will have to know the SSID before they can authenticate and associate with the access point. When SSID broadcasting is disabled, the client sends a probe request with the configured SSID and the access point with the matching SSID responds. While this is more secure than broadcasting, the probe requests are sent in clear text and can be seen using a product such as AiroPeek. Therefore, SSIDs are never to be considered a security method. They can, however, be used in a more secure manner, and that is the purpose of this lab.

In this lab, you will capture packets and view the broadcast SSIDs using AiroPeek. You will then disable SSID broadcasting. Using AiroPeek again, you will view the probe request and probe response frames that are necessary when SSID broadcasting is disabled.

After completing this lab, you will be able to:

➤ Understand when SSID broadcasting should be disabled

➤ Disable SSID broadcasting

➤ Define probe response and probe request

Materials Required

This lab requires the following for each team:

➤ Two laptop computers running Windows XP and configured with a Cisco Aironet adapter

➤ Cisco 1200 series access point

➤ One UTP patch cable

➤ Power cable for the access point

➤ Access to the wired network through a switch (only one switch is required, regardless of the number of teams)

➤ Completion of the Chapter 2 labs

8

Estimated completion time: **30 minutes**

ACTIVITY

NOTE

This lab assumes that you have completed Lab 5.5, which installed a program called AiroPeek. If you did not complete Lab 5.5, you can still do this lab, but you must complete Steps 1 through 27 of Lab 5.5 to download and install AiroPeek first.

1. Connect and power up your access point if necessary. Make sure it is connected to the switch. Turn on your laptops and log in.

2. Point to the ADU icon in the tray. Your laptops should be using the Infrastructure Mode profile and should be associated to your own access point. You will be using AiroPeek to monitor SSID broadcasting and Internet Explorer to configure the access point.

3. On the non-AiroPeek computer, open the **Aironet Desktop Utility**. Click the **Current Status** tab if necessary. What channel are you using?

   _____

   Leave the window open.

4. On the AiroPeek computer, click **Start**, point to **All Programs**, and click **WildPackets AiroPeek Demo** to open the AiroPeek program. Click **OK** to launch the program.

5. Click **File** and then click **New**. Click the **802.11** tab and use the list box to select the channel you recorded in Step 3 in the **Number** text box, if necessary.

6. Click the **Filters** tab. Select **802.11 Management** frames. Management frames include frames used to authenticate and associate with a wireless access point. Beacons are included in this category. Click **OK**.

7. In AiroPeek, click the **Start Capture** button. The demo will capture up to 250 packets for up to 30 seconds. Click **OK** when the capture ends. The Monitor Statistics function, which started automatically when you opened AiroPeek, will also end at some point. When you see the notification window, click **OK** and continue with the lab.

8. Scroll to the right in the capture window and double-click any beacon frame. Scroll down to the SSID section of the window. Can you see your SSID?

   _____

9. Close the packet window but do not close the AiroPeek program.

10. Open Internet Explorer on the non-AiroPeek laptop. Browse to your access point. You will need the IP address of your access point, which you configured in Step 15 of Lab 2.2. Log in as **administrator** with the password **Cisco**.

11. Click **Security**. Click **SSID Manager**. Click your **SSID**. Scroll to the bottom of the window and notice that your SSID is operating in guest mode. What does guest mode mean?

    _____

12. Change the Set Guest Mode SSID to **<NONE>** using the list box. Click **Apply** and then click **OK**. Close Internet Explorer.

13. On the AiroPeek laptop, click **File** and then click **New**. Click the **802.11** tab and make sure the channel you recorded in Step 3 is listed in the **Number** text box.

14. Click the **Filters** tab. Select **802.11 Management** packets. Click **OK**. Do not click the Start Capture button yet.

15. On the non-AiroPeek laptop, click the **Profile Management** tab in the Aironet Desktop Utility program window. Change the profile to **Ad Hoc Mode** by double-clicking it. The ADU icon in the tray turns gray, indicating you have lost connectivity.

16. Next, click the **Start Capture** button in AiroPeek and then quickly double-click the **Infrastructure Mode** profile on the non-AiroPeek laptop. The purpose is to capture authentication and association packets.

17. When the capture stops, click **OK** on the AiroPeek laptop and scroll to the right to find a beacon packet. Double-click a **beacon packet** associated with your access point, which is identified by its MAC address listed in the Source column. Scroll down to the SSID section. Can you see your SSID?

    _____

    Why or why not?

    _____

    Close the packet window but don't close AiroPeek.

18. Double-click a **probe request** (Probe Req) frame that indicates SSID information in the Summary column. Scroll down to the SSID section. Can you see the SSID? _____

    What are the clients doing now that they didn't have to do before you disabled guest mode for your SSID?

    _____

    Regarding the current configuration on your access point, do clients have to know the SSID to associate? _____

    Close the packet window but don't close AiroPeek.

19. Double-click a **probe response** (Probe Rsp) frame. Can you see the SSID in the probe response frame? _____

20. Close the AiroPeek program.

21. Close all windows and shut down the laptops.

Certification Objectives

Objectives for the CWNA exam:

➤ Describe the types of wireless LAN security attacks, and explain how to identify and prevent them

Review Questions

1. When is it appropriate to use SSID broadcasting?

2. What type of management frames are used to associate with an access point when SSID broadcasting is disabled?

3. Why is disabling SSIDs not considered a security solution?

4. SSIDs do not appear in a probe response or a probe request. True or False?

5. SSIDs do not appear in beacons when SSID broadcasting is disabled. True or False?

Lab 8.4 Spoofing a MAC Address

Objectives

Most of us think of MAC addresses as unchangeable, permanent, physical addresses because they are burned into the network adapter. Technically, the burned-in address (BIA) may not be the same as the MAC address used in the MAC header. As it turns out, nearly all 802.11 cards in use permit their MAC addresses to be altered, often with full support from the drivers. Windows users are commonly permitted to change their MAC address by selecting the properties of their network card. MAC addresses of wireless access points and clients are broadcast in clear text even when WEP encryption is used. Thus, an attacker may choose to alter his MAC address to match the MAC address of a legitimate client. There may be several reasons for doing this, including evading detection by intrusion detection systems and bypassing MAC filtering mechanisms. When spoofing a MAC address, it is important that hackers wait until the legitimate MAC address is no longer in use on the network, because duplicate MAC addresses on the same network are usually unable to communicate. The purpose of this lab is to show you how to spoof a MAC address and associate to the Linksys router using the spoofed address.

In this lab, you will change the MAC address on one of the laptops to match the MAC address on the other laptop. You will then associate with the Linksys wireless "G" router using the spoofed address. Finally, you will reconfigure the laptop to use its BIA as its MAC address.

After completing this lab, you will be able to:

➤ Spoof a MAC address

➤ Understand why MAC filtering is not an effective security measure

Materials Required

This lab requires the following for each team:

➤ Two laptop computers running Windows XP and configured with a Cisco Aironet adapter

➤ One Linksys wireless "G" router

➤ Power cable for the wireless router

➤ Completion of Labs 2.1, 2.5, and 3.4

Estimated completion time: **20 minutes**

ACTIVITY

1. Connect and power up your Linksys router if necessary. Turn on your laptops. Make sure your laptops are using the **Infrastructure Mode** profile and are connected to the Linksys router.

2. On both laptops, open a command prompt window by clicking **Start**, then clicking **Run**. Type **cmd** and press **Enter**.

3. Enter the **ipconfig /all** command on both laptops, and record the IP and corresponding MAC addresses for the wireless network adapter for both laptops in Table 8-1. Include the name of the computer. Make sure all team members record the computers in the same order. Close the command prompt window.

Table 8-1   Client laptop IP and MAC addresses

Laptop Number	Computer Name	IP Address	MAC Address
1.			
2.			

4. You will now configure laptop 2 to use laptop 1's MAC address. On laptop 2, click **Start**, click **Control Panel**, click **Network and Internet Connections**, and then click **Network Connections**.

5. Right-click **Cisco Wireless Adapter** and click **Properties**.

6. On the **General** tab, click the **Configure** button.

7. Click the **Advanced** tab and click **Network Address**.

8. Click in the **Value** text box and enter the MAC address of laptop 1 that you recorded in Table 8-1. Don't use any separators such as colons or periods.

9. Make sure the **Value** text box is selected rather than Not Present and click **OK**. Did you lose your wireless connection to the access point? _____

   Is laptop 1 still connected? _____

10. On laptop 2, open a command prompt window again and enter the **ipconfig /all** command. Does the MAC address of laptop 1 appear to be the physical address of laptop 2? _____

You should have answered Yes. If you answered No, close the command prompt window, reopen it, and enter the **ipconfig/all** command again. Close the command prompt window.

11. On laptop 1, open the command prompt window again and enter the **ipconfig /all** command. Is the MAC address of the wireless adapter on this laptop the same as the one displayed on laptop 2? _____

    Why do you think you lost your connection to the access point on laptop 2 but not on laptop 1?

    _____

    Close the command prompt window.

12. Shut down laptop 1 and restart laptop 2. Once restarted, laptop 2 should connect to the Linksys wireless "G" router using the Infrastructure Mode profile. Point to the ADU icon in the tray to make sure your laptop is connected.

13. On laptop 2, open the command prompt window and enter the **ipconfig /all** command. The MAC address listed for the wireless adapter should match the MAC address you listed in Table 8-1. Laptop 2 is connected to the wireless router using laptop 1's MAC address. This is an example of spoofing. Close the command prompt window.

14. You will now configure laptop 2 to use its own BIA. On laptop 2, click **Start**, click **Control Panel**, click **Network and Internet Connections**, and then click **Network Connections**.

15. Right-click **Cisco Wireless Adapter** and click **Properties**.

16. On the **General** tab, click the **Configure** button.

17. Click the **Advanced** tab and click **Network Address**.

18. Select **Not Present** and click **OK**.

19. Open a command prompt window and enter the **ipconfig /all** command. Your MAC address for the wireless adapter should match the one recorded in Table 8-1 for laptop 2.

20. Shut down the laptop.

Certification Objectives

Objectives for the CWNA exam:

➤ Identify the strengths, weaknesses, and appropriate uses of wireless LAN security techniques

➤ Describe the types of wireless LAN security attacks, and explain how to identify and prevent them

Review Questions

1. The BIA and the MAC address are typically the same. True or False?

2. What is the difference between the BIA and the MAC address?

3. MAC address filtering is considered to be a security option on small wireless networks. What is your opinion regarding this security option?

4. Will WEP encryption prevent MAC spoofing? Why or why not?

5. Two computers using the same MAC address on the same network can usually communicate simultaneously. True or False?

8

IMPLEMENTING WIRELESS LAN SECURITY

Labs included in this chapter

➤ Lab 9.1 Creating and Applying an IP Filter

➤ Lab 9.2 Configuring the Temporal Key Integrity Protocol

➤ Lab 9.3 Replacing Telnet with SSH

➤ Lab 9.4 Wardriving

CWNA Exam Objectives	
Objective	Lab
Identify the strengths, weaknesses, and appropriate uses of wireless LAN security techniques	9.1, 9.2
Describe the types of wireless LAN security attacks, and explain how to identify and prevent them	9.3, 9.4

LAB 9.1 CREATING AND APPLYING AN IP FILTER

Objectives

In Lab 8.1, you created a MAC filter to block all but one particular client. MAC filters are commonly used on wireless home networks. IP filters are less commonly used on home networks, but can be a very important addition to SOHO and even larger wireless networks. Like MAC filters, IP filters are a type of access list. IP filters prevent or allow the use of specific protocols, ports, or addresses through the access point's Ethernet and radio ports. You can create a filter that passes all traffic except what you specify, or alternatively, a filter that blocks all traffic except the traffic you specify. You can create filters that contain elements of one, two, or all three IP filtering methods. You can apply the filters you create to either or both the Ethernet and radio ports, and to either or both incoming and outgoing packets. IP filters are not only a security feature but an excellent way to control utilization of bandwidth. The purpose of this lab is to learn how to create and apply IP filters on a Cisco 1200 series access point.

In this lab, you will create an IP filter that blocks Telnet, SNMP, Internet Relay Chat, and rlogin while permitting all other types of traffic. You will then apply the filter incoming to the radio interface on your access point. Finally, you will test the filter and then delete it.

After completing this lab, you will be able to:

➤ Understand how to create and apply an IP filter

Materials Required

This lab requires the following for each team:

➤ Two laptop computers running Windows XP and configured with a Cisco Aironet adapter

➤ One Cisco Aironet 1200 access point using IOS-based firmware and interface

➤ One UTP patch cable

➤ Power cable for the access point

➤ Access to the wired network through a switch

➤ Completion of the Chapter 2 labs

Estimated completion time: **20 minutes**

ACTIVITY

1. Connect and power up your access point if necessary. Turn on your laptops. Make sure your laptops are using the **Infrastructure Mode** profile.

2. On one laptop, browse to your access point using Internet Explorer. You will need the IP address of your access point. The IP addresses are listed in Table 2-4 of Lab 2.2. Log on as a valid user.

3. Click **Services** in the left pane. Click **Filters**, then click the **IP Filters** tab.

4. In the Filter Name field, enter **securityfilter** and change the Default Action to **Forward all**.

5. Scroll down to the **UDP/TCP Port** section and select **Internet Relay Chat (194)** from the TCP Port list box. Choose **Block** for the Action and then click **Add**.

6. Repeat Step 5 for **Telnet (23)** and **Login (rlogin, 513).**

7. In the UDP Port section, choose **Simple Network Management Protocol (161)** from the list box. Choose **Block** for the Action and then click **Add**.

8. Scroll down to see your list. There should be five entries, including Default – Forward all at the bottom of the list. The Forward All statement is necessary because each packet processed through an access list must match a line in the access list; otherwise, the packet will be denied. Click **Apply**, then click **OK**.

9. Click the **Apply Filters** tab at the top of the window. Select **securityfilter** from the list box in the **incoming** row of the **Radio0-802.11G** column. Click **Apply**, then click **OK** to apply the list.

10. On the other laptop, navigate to the command prompt window and telnet to your access point using the **telnet [ip of access point]** command. What was the response?

    _____

    Does your filter appear to be working? _____

    You should *not* have been able to telnet. If your telnet attempt was successful, return to the Cisco IOS browser, click **System Software**, click **System Configuration**, and then click **Restart** to restart the access point. Once the access point reloads, telnetting to the access point via the radio interface should be unsuccessful.

11. In the Filters window of the Cisco IOS browser, click the **Apply Filters** tab, if necessary. Change the filter applied to the radio interface from securityfilter back to **<NONE>**. Click **Apply** and then click **OK**.

12. Once again, on the other laptop, navigate to the command prompt window and telnet to your access point using the **telnet [ip of access point]** command. Were you able to telnet successfully to your access point? _____

Did you remove the list or just the application of the list in Step 11?

_____

13. Click the **IP Filters** tab. Make sure **securityfilter** is listed in the **Filter Name** text box. Scroll down, click the **Delete** button at the bottom of the screen, and then click **OK** to delete the filter. It should no longer be in the Filter Name text box.

14. Close all windows and shut down the laptops.

Certification Objectives

Objectives for the CWNA exam:

➤ Identify the strengths, weaknesses, and appropriate uses of wireless LAN security techniques

Review Questions

1. What three parameters can you filter on using an IP filter on a Cisco 1200 series access point?

2. A configured filter doesn't work unless it is applied to an interface. True or False?

3. IP filters can only be applied as incoming filters. True or False?

4. IP filters provide some security. What other important function can IP filters provide?

5. In Step 8 you viewed the filter you created. There were five entries, one of which was Forward all. Why is the Forward all statement necessary at the end of the access list?

LAB 9.2 CONFIGURING THE TEMPORAL KEY INTEGRITY PROTOCOL

Objectives

In Lab 8.2, you configured static WEP. WEP is considered to be a very low level of security. The big security hole with static WEP is the initialization vector (IV), which is sent in clear text with every packet. If you collect enough packets using a packet sniffer, the IVs start repeating. This provides a way for hackers to break your WEP key. The Temporal Key Integrity Protocol (TKIP) is a suite of algorithms that adds security enhancements to WEP. Cisco Aironet access points and client adapters support both Cisco's proprietary version of TKIP and the Wi-Fi Protected Access (WPA) version, although WPA is preferred. TKIP defeats weak-key attacks and detects replay attacks by providing fresh keys to WEP, which makes it impossible to break WEP keys by collecting large amounts of packets. The IV is still visible in clear text, but it doesn't matter because the key stream is always unique. TKIP is not a long-term security solution, but it is a big improvement over static WEP. The Advanced Encryption Standard (AES), which uses the more robust Rijndael algorithm, will replace TKIP and WEP. TKIP uses the RC4 symmetric algorithm just like WEP. The purpose of this lab is to learn how to configure TKIP on the Cisco 1200 series access point.

In this lab, you will configure your access point to use TKIP with 128-bit WEP encryption. You will then reconfigure your Open Authentication with WEP profile to use the same 128-bit WEP key so that you can connect to your wireless network using TKIP. Finally, you will remove these security settings.

After completing this lab, you will be able to:

➤ Configure TKIP with 128-bit WEP on the Cisco 1200 access point

➤ Modify a client profile for 128-bit WEP

Materials Required

This lab requires the following for each team:

➤ Two laptop computers running Windows XP and configured with a Cisco Aironet adapter

➤ One Cisco Aironet 1200 access point using IOS-based firmware and interface

➤ One UTP patch cable

➤ Power cable for the access point

➤ Access to the wired network through a switch

➤ Completion of the Chapter 2 labs

Estimated completion time: **45 minutes**

ACTIVITY

NOTE

This lab assumes that you have completed Lab 8.2, which created a client profile named Open Authentication with WEP. If you did not complete Lab 8.2, you can still do this lab, but you must complete Steps 9 and 10 of Lab 8.2 first.

1. Connect and power up your team's access point if necessary. Turn on both of your laptops and log in. You should be using the **Infrastructure Mode** profile.

2. Open Internet Explorer on one laptop. Browse to your access point using its IP address, as recorded in Table 2-4 of Lab 2.2, and log on using a valid user-name and password.

3. Click **Security**, then click **Encryption Manager**.

4. In the **Encryption Modes** section, select **Cipher**, then select **TKIP + WEP 128 bit** from the list box.

5. Scroll down to the **Encryption Key** section and select **Encryption Key 1** as the Transmit Key. Select **128 bit** for the key size. Enter **0123456789ABCDEF0123456789**. Be very careful when entering the key. You may want to type it in Notepad where you can see it and then cut and paste it to the Encryption Key text box. Alternatively, you can record it on a piece of paper just to make sure you didn't make a typing error. Make sure the letters are in uppercase.

6. Scroll down and click **Apply**, then click **OK**. In a few seconds, you will lose connectivity. Minimize Internet Explorer.

7. On both computers, open the **Aironet Desktop Utility** from the shortcut on the desktop.

8. Click the **Profile Management** tab, if necessary.

9. Click the **Open Authentication with WEP** profile and then click the **Modify** button.

10. Click the **Security** tab. Notice that Pre-Shared Key is selected. Click the **Configure** button. The WEP Key 1 as entered is a 40-bit key. Click the option button in the 128 column to select a **128 bit** WEP key size. Change the key to **0123456789ABCDEF0123456789** to match the key on your access point and click **OK**.

11. Click **OK** again, then double-click the **Open Authentication with WEP** profile to activate it. In a few seconds, you should reconnect.

12. Click **Start** and then click **Run**. Type **cmd** and press **Enter** to access the command prompt window.

13. Enter the **telnet** command followed by the IP address of your access point. Log on with the username **Cisco** and the password **Cisco**.

14. Type **enable** and press **Enter**. When prompted for the enable password, enter **Cisco**.

15. Enter the **show run** command and use the Spacebar to scroll down until you get to the Dot11Radio0 section. Notice that TKIP and 128-bit WEP have been configured.

16. Return to the IOS browser window in Internet Explorer. You might be required to browse to it using the IP address of your access point. Click **Security**, then click **Encryption Manager**, if necessary.

17. In the **Encryption Modes** section, select **None** to remove the encryption. Scroll down and click **Apply**, then click **OK**. In a few seconds you will lose connectivity.

18. On both laptops, open the **Aironet Desktop Utility**, if necessary, and double-click the **Infrastructure Mode** profile on the **Profile Management** tab to activate it. You should reconnect.

19. Shut down the laptops.

Certification Objectives

Objectives for the CWNA exam:

➤ Identify the strengths, weaknesses, and appropriate uses of wireless LAN security techniques

Review Questions

1. TKIP is a long-term security solution. True or False?

2. What will be the replacement for TKIP and WEP?

3. What algorithm does TKIP and WEP use?

4. TKIP improves on WEP's weaknesses by encrypting the IV. True or False?

5. How does TKIP enhance WEP?

LAB 9.3 REPLACING TELNET WITH SSH

Objectives

SSH is a multipurpose program that allows you to access systems remotely and execute commands on those remote systems in a cryptographically secure way. You can even move files and check e-mail with SSH. SSH provides authentication and encryption over insecure channels and is recommended on both wired and wireless systems, as a replacement for rlogin, FTP, Telnet, and other insecure remote access protocols. All of these remote access protocols work at the Application layer, but SSH is the only one that offers authentication and encryption. SSH uses connection-oriented transport on port 22. SSH uses the same usernames and passwords allowed by the Telnet program and provides the same functionality as Telnet with the added benefits of security. As for the client side, many new computers have the SSH client installed. In this lab you will download a free SSH client named Putty that is easy to use. The purpose of this lab is to understand how to implement SSH, which provides a secure alternative to Telnet.

In this lab you will configure your access point to use SSH, download and configure the SSH client Putty on both laptops, and then connect to your access point using SSH.

After completing this lab, you will be able to:

➤ Understand why SSH is preferred over Telnet for remote communications

➤ Configure SSH on a Cisco 1200 series access point as well as the laptops

Materials Required

This lab requires the following for each team:

➤ Two laptop computers running Windows XP and configured with a Cisco Aironet adapter

➤ Cisco 1200 series access point

➤ One UTP patch cable

➤ Power cable for the access point

➤ Access to the wired network through a switch (only one switch is required, regardless of the number of teams)

➤ Completion of the Chapter 2 labs

Estimated completion time: **20 minutes**

This lab depends on Putty's Web site, which may have changed slightly since the writing of this lab.

NOTE

ACTIVITY

LAB ACTIVITY

1. Connect and power up your team's access point if necessary. Turn on both of your laptops and log on. You should be connected using the **Infrastructure Mode** profile before continuing.

2. On one laptop, open Internet Explorer. Browse to your access point using the administrator account. The password is **Cisco**.

3. Click **Services** and then click **Telnet/SSH**.

4. Scroll down to Secure Shell and click the **Enabled** button.

5. In the System Name text box, enter your **team name** (for example, echo-foxtrot). Your team name may already be listed.

6. In the Domain Name text box, enter your **team name**.

7. Enter **512** for the RSA Key Size. Click **Apply** and then click **OK**. Your access point is ready to accept SSH conversations.

8. You will download and install Putty on both laptops. Open Internet Explorer and browse to **www.chiark.greenend.org.uk/~sgtatham/putty/download.html**.

9. Click **putty.exe** in the "Windows 95, 98, ME, NT, 2000, and XP on Intel x86" section. Save the installation to the desktop.

10. On both laptops, navigate to the desktop and then double-click **Putty** to open the program. In the Host Name (or IP address) text box, enter the IP address of your access point. Make sure **22** is listed as the port number and that the selected protocol is **SSH**.

11. Click **Open**. The first time you open the program you will be given a warning. Read the warning. Click **Yes** to add the RSA key to Putty's cache.

12. Putty opens and displays a command-line interface that prompts you to log on. Log on with the username **Cisco**. The password also is **Cisco**. This is the same default username and password when using Telnet with the Cisco 1200 series access point. What is the prompt? _____

13. Type **enable** and press **Enter** to access privileged exec mode. Enter the password, which is **Cisco**. What is the prompt? _____

14. Enter the **show run** command. Press the Spacebar to scroll through the text. With respect to interface and functionality, how does Putty's SSH program compare to Windows' Telnet program?

_____

9

15. Enter the **logout** command. In addition to logging out of the SSH session, what else does the Putty program do when the logout command is issued?

_____

16. Shut down the laptops.

Certification Objectives

Objectives for the CWNA exam:

➤ Describe the types of wireless LAN security attacks, and explain how to identify and prevent them

Review Questions

1. With respect to today's security environment, what is the problem with using FTP and Telnet for remote access?

2. What is the port number for SSH, and does it use connectionless or connection-oriented transport?

3. At which layer of the OSI model do FTP, Telnet, and SSH operate?

4. SSH provides secure data communications but does not provide secure authentication. True or False?

5. By default, your SSH login and password will be the same as the one used for Telnet. True or False?

LAB 9.4 WARDRIVING

Objectives

Wardriving is the gathering of statistics about wireless networks in a given area. There are various programs that listen for beacons broadcast by access points or probes transmitted by laptops, but Network Stumbler (also known as NetStumbler) is by far the most popular program for this activity. Wardriving is fun, like a scavenger hunt, and it provides information regarding the types of systems and configurations in use. As you will see, most configurations are not secure. Wardriving is not illegal; however, actually connecting to a non-public access point without the owner's permission *is* illegal. Although many wardrivers add extra equipment to their laptops such as external antennas, pigtail cables, GPS receivers, and power adapters for the cigarette lighters, your laptop with its standard wireless adapter and built-in antenna should work just fine. Many wardrivers leave symbols for other wardrivers to help them connect (illegally) to a nearby wireless system. This process is known as warchalking. Warchalking symbols are varied but usually include symbols for open node, closed node, and WEP node. Open node means that the access point is in guest mode and is broadcasting the SSID. Closed node means that the SSID is not being broadcast by the access point, so a sniffer such as AiroPeek or AirMagnet is required to detect it. WEP node means that communications are being encrypted using a WEP key. The purpose of this lab is to investigate the wireless systems in use in a neighborhood.

In this lab, you and your team will wardrive in a specific neighborhood using the Network Stumbler program. You will record the MAC address, SSID, channel assignment, link speed, equipment vendor, and encryption method for the access points you detect. You also will record the appropriate warchalking symbol.

After completing this lab, you will be able to:

➤ Use the Network Stumbler program to wardrive

➤ Understand how hackers can steal bandwidth so easily

➤ Recognize common warchalking symbols

Materials Required

This lab requires the following for each team:

➤ One laptop computer running Windows XP and configured with a Cisco Aironet adapter

➤ The Network Stumbler program installed on the laptop

➤ Map of nearby neighborhoods

➤ Completion of the Chapter 2 labs

Estimated completion time: **45 minutes**

NOTE

In Lab 7.3, you downloaded the Network Stumbler program on one of the team laptops. If you did not complete Lab 7.3, you can still do this lab, but you must complete Steps 2 and 3 of Lab 7.3 first.

LAB ACTIVITY

ACTIVITY

1. You will be using the laptop on which you downloaded Network Stumbler in Lab 7.3. If the laptop you are using belongs to another entity, such as a school, you may need to complete and sign a field trip permission form, which specifies that you are signing out a laptop and are completely responsible for it. Each team member should sign a form and submit the form to the instructor.

2. Turn on the Network Stumbler laptop and double-click the **Aironet Desktop Utility** shortcut to open it. Click the **Profile Management** tab, if necessary. Click the **Infrastructure Mode** profile and click the **Modify** button. Your SSID should be configured in the SSID 1 text box. If it isn't configured, configure it now and click **OK**. This will prevent your laptop from connecting with any access point that doesn't have this SSID. Remember, connecting to a non-public access point without permission is illegal.

3. Shut down the laptop.

4. Determine which of your team members will be driving the car for your team. This person must have a valid driver's license and registration.

5. The wardriving neighborhood for each team is listed in Table 9-1. Locate your wardriving neighborhood on the map provided by your instructor.

Table 9-1   Nearby wardriving neighborhoods

Team Name	Nearby Neighborhood
alpha-bravo	
charlie-delta	
echo-foxtrot	
golf-hotel	
india-juliet	

6. Take this lab, a pencil, and the laptop with Network Stumbler on it to the car. The car owner should drive. The team member with the laptop should sit in the front passenger seat. Other team members should sit in the back seat with this lab sheet and pencil and record lab results.

7. Drive directly to your assigned neighborhood with the laptop off. When you get to the neighborhood, find a good place to pull over. You should not pull into a person's private driveway.

8. Turn on the laptop. Log on and open the Network Stumbler program. Maximize both Network Stumbler windows.

9. When Network Stumbler detects an access point, you should hear a sound and the access point should appear in the Network Stumbler window. You may want to open the car windows, but this should not be necessary to detect access points.

10. If you do not detect any access points, begin to drive slowly through the neighborhood. When you get a "hit," pull over and park again.

11. For each access point detected, record the parameters in Table 9-2. Warchalking symbols are shown in Figure 9-1. Attempt to record information for at least six access points.

9

Table 9-2   Wardriving parameters

MAC Address	SSID	Channel	Link Speed	Equipment Vendor	Encryption	Warchalking Symbol

Figure 9-1   Warchalking symbols

12. When you are finished recording information, close the Network Stumbler program. You will be prompted to save the file. Click **Yes** to save the changes. Save the file in My Documents using the neighborhood name in Table 9-1 as the filename.

13. Shut down the laptop. Drive directly back to the school and bring the laptop and lab sheets back into the classroom.

Certification Objectives

Objectives for the CWNA exam:

➤ Describe the types of wireless LAN security attacks, and explain how to identify and prevent them

Review Questions

1. Approximately what percentage of the access points that you detected in the activity were using 54-Mbps technology?

2. Approximately what percentage of the access points that you detected were using WEP or some other type of encryption?

3. Approximately what percentage of the access points that you detected were not broadcasting their SSIDs (closed networks)?

4. How could you find out the SSID for a closed network?

5. Why do you think it is illegal to connect to a non-public wireless network that you come across while wardriving?

CHAPTER TEN

MANAGING A WIRELESS LAN

Labs included in this chapter

➤ Lab 10.1 Defining Common Wireless LAN Accessories

➤ Lab 10.2 Creating Wireless User Accounts

➤ Lab 10.3 Investigating the Cisco Discovery Protocol

CWNA Exam Objectives	
Objective	**Lab**
Identify the use of wireless LAN accessories	10.1
Labs 10.2 and 10.3 do not map to a certification objective; however, they contain information that will be beneficial to your professional development.	

Lab 10.1 Defining Common Wireless LAN Accessories

Objectives

On most occasions, your access point will be a stand-alone unit. You will simply attach the antennas and start configuring the device. Sometimes, however, and especially when outdoor antenna placement is required, you will need to purchase and install additional equipment. This equipment, which is known as wireless LAN accessories, includes amplifiers, attenuators, lightning arrestors, splitters, various cables and connectors, frequency converters, Power over Ethernet (PoE) devices, and bandwidth control units. Whenever you add accessories to your main system, be sure the accessories have the same impedance rating in order to avoid Voltage Standing Wave Ratio (VSWR) problems. VSWR can cause unstable power conditions as well as radio transmitter burnout. The typical impedance on data networks is 50 ohms. It is important to understand the role that wireless LAN accessories play in your wireless LAN system. The purpose of this lab is to help you learn the terminology and definitions associated with these accessories.

In this lab, you will match the correct wireless LAN accessory with a definition.

After completing this lab, you will be able to:

➤ Define various wireless LAN accessories

Materials Required

This lab requires the following:

➤ Internet access

➤ Pencil or pen

Estimated completion time: **30 minutes**

Activity

Match each term in the following bulleted list with a definition in the numbered list. A term may be used more than once. Use the Internet and Web sites such as *www.whatis.com* and *www.webopedia.com* if you need to search for a definition.

➤ Amplifier

➤ ~~Splitter~~

➤ ~~PoE~~

➤ Attenuator

➤ Pigtail

➤ Bandwidth control unit

➤ Lightning arrestor

➤ Frequency converter

➤ BNC, TNC, and SMA

1. One end has a proprietary connector and the other has an industry-standard connector.
   _____

2. May be used to keep track of power output by connecting a power meter to one output and an RF antenna to the other.
   _____

3. Used to introduce gain into an RF system.
   _____

4. Used to switch from one frequency range to another.
   _____

5. Shunts transient current to ground. _____

6. Used to introduce loss into an RF system. _____

7. Especially useful when no power outlet is located in the area where you want to place your access point.
   ____PoE____

8. Has a single input connector and multiple output connectors.
   ____Splitter____

9. This system requires an active switch or a power injector.
   _____

10. Especially useful when the frequency range you are using is congested.
    _____

11. May be necessary if your power output is above FCC regulations.
    _____

12. Typically filter on MAC addresses to put a user in an assigned queue with particular properties. _____

13. Will not protect your system from a direct lightning strike. _____

14. Industry-standard connectors used on wireless LANs.
    _____

15. A type of adapter.
    _____

16. Used to conserve and protect bandwidth. _____

10

Certification Objectives

Objectives for the CWNA exam:

➤ Identify the use of wireless LAN accessories

Review Questions

1. Under what conditions would you need a pigtail cable?

2. Which two accessories are used to control the power output in a wireless system?

3. What is the purpose of using PoE? *allows the electrical current to be carried by Data cables.*

4. Why is it important that all accessories added to a wireless system have the same impedance?

5. What types of problems are caused by VSWR?

Lab 10.2 Creating Wireless User Accounts

Objectives

Up to this point, when using Internet Explorer, you have been configuring your wireless access point using the default administrative user account. When using this browser interface, you have been logging on as administrator with the password Cisco. As you will see in this lab, the default administrator account will accept any username, even no username, as long as the password is Cisco. Regarding Telnet, the default username is Cisco and the password is Cisco. You can make remote access point configuration more secure by creating specific user accounts and disabling the default administrator account. The purpose of this lab is to learn how to create user accounts.

In this lab, you will explore the effects of creating user accounts for all of your teammates, then forcing the access point only to accept entry using those accounts. You also will create a host name for your access point.

After completing this lab, you will be able to:

➤ Create user accounts on the Cisco 1200 access point

➤ Disable the default administrator account

➤ Configure a new host name for your access point

Materials Required

This lab requires the following:

➤ Two laptop computers running Windows XP and configured with a Cisco Aironet adapter

➤ One Cisco Aironet 1200 access point using IOS-based firmware and interface

➤ One UTP patch cable

➤ Power cable for the access point

➤ Access to the wired network through a switch

➤ Completion of the Chapter 2 labs

10

Estimated completion time: **30 minutes**

ACTIVITY

1. Connect and power up your access point if necessary. Make sure it is connected to the switch. Turn on your laptops and log on.

2. Point to the ADU icon in the tray. Your laptops should be using the Infrastructure Mode profile. If you are not using this profile, open the Aironet Desktop Utility program and activate the **Infrastructure Mode** profile.

3. On both laptops, open Internet Explorer. Browse to your access point using its IP address. The IP addresses are listed in Table 2-4 in Lab 2.2. The username is **administrator**. The password is **Cisco**.

4. Close Internet Explorer. Reopen it and browse to your access point. This time, though, do not enter anything for the username. Enter **Cisco** as usual for the password. Were you able to gain access without logging on as a specific user? _____

5. On both laptops, open a command prompt window and enter the **telnet [ip address of the access point]** command to telnet to your access point. When prompted for the username, just press **Enter** without entering one. Were you able to telnet without a username? _____

   Enter **Cisco** for the username and **Cisco** for the password. This is the default login for Telnet on the Cisco 1200 series access point.

6. Type **enable** at the user mode prompt and press **Enter**. You will be prompted for an enable mode password. Type **Cisco** and press **Enter**. You should now be at the privileged mode prompt. Enter the **logout** command to exit Telnet.

7. On one laptop only, return to the Internet Explorer window, and then click **EXPRESS SET-UP**. If you completed Lab 9.3, you configured a host name (system name) for your access point. What is the system name for your access point? _____

   If the system name is ap, no host name was configured, because ap is the default system name on the Cisco 1200 series access point.

8. If your system name is your team name, skip to Step 9. If your system name is ap, type your team name (for example, alpha-bravo) in the System Name text box. Scroll down and click **Apply**, then click **OK**.

9. Click **SECURITY** and then click **Admin Access**. Scroll down to the **Local User List (Individual Passwords)** area. There is a default user named Cisco. Click **Cisco** and notice that this user has Read-Only access. You will add each of your team members as users with Read-Write access.

10. Click **<NEW>**, then type a username in the Username text box, using the format of first initial plus last name (for example, kcannon). Although it is not secure, for this lab you should enter **password** in the Password text box. Enter the same password in the Confirm Password text box, and then select the **Read-Write** option. The Cisco IOS mandates that at least one user has Read-Write privileges. This is equivalent to administrator-level access. Click **Apply** and then click **OK**.

11. Repeat Step 10 for all users on your team.

12. Scroll up and select **Local User List Only (Individual Passwords)**. This will disable the default administrator account and allow only the users in the local list to access your access point. Click the appropriate **Apply** button, click **OK**, and then click **OK** again.

13. At some point you will be disconnected because the user you logged on as is no longer authenticated. After you are disconnected, try logging on as **administrator** with the password **Cisco**. Did it work? _____

   If it didn't work, you have successfully disabled the default administrator account.

14. Log on using one of your new user accounts. You should be successful. Were you successful? _____

15. Click **SECURITY** in the left pane. You should see the default Cisco Read-Only account and the new Read-Write accounts that have been configured for your teammates. Figure 10-1 shows an example of this configuration.

16. On the other laptop, attempt another Telnet session with your access point. Try logging on using the default username **Cisco** and the password **Cisco**. Notice that it appears to work and you get to the user mode prompt (>).

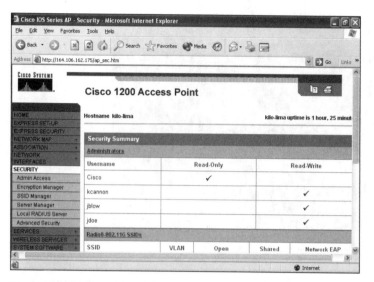

Figure 10-1   Security summary

17. Type **enable** and press **Enter** to get to privileged exec mode. What message do you get?

_____

18. At the user mode prompt, enter the **show run** command. Did it work?

_____

The show run command displays the configuration of the access point and warrants a higher level of access. This command only can be issued in privileged (enable) mode, and the Cisco user account does not permit that level of access.

19. At the user mode prompt, enter the **show clock** command. Did it work?

_____

This is considered a low-level command in terms of security, so you can use it in user mode.

20. Enter the **logout** command and attempt another Telnet session using one of the new user accounts. Were you required to enter an enable mode password to get to privileged mode? _____

Your accounts were configured for Read-Write access, which is administrator-level access, so no enable password is required.

21. In the command prompt window, enter the **show run** command. You should see the Cisco account as well as your new accounts. Notice that the new Read-Write accounts have a security level of 15. This is the highest level of security on Cisco access points and switches. Figure 10-2 displays part of the Telnet command output for kilo-lima.

10

```
Current configuration : 2275 bytes
!
version 12.2
no service pad
service timestamps debug datetime msec
service timestamps log datetime msec
service password-encryption
!
hostname kilo-lima
!
logging queue-limit 100
!
username Cisco password 7 047802150C2E
username kcannon privilege 15 password 7 051B071C325B411B1D
username jblow privilege 15 password 7 0216054818110003348
username jdoe privilege 15 password 7 08314D5D1A0E0A0516
ip subnet-zero
ip domain name kilo-lima
!
aaa new-model
!
!
aaa group server radius rad_eap
 --More--
```

Figure 10-2   Show run output

22. Press the Spacebar to scroll through the output, then type **logout** and press **Enter** to exit the Telnet session.

23. Close all windows and shut down the laptops.

Certification Objectives

This lab does not map to a certification objective; however, it contains information that will be beneficial to your professional development.

Review Questions

1. What is the default administrator username and password on the Cisco 1200 series access point?

2. What is the default Telnet username and password on the Cisco 1200 series access point?

3. How does user management via the Local User List Only option increase security?

4. In terms of security levels on Cisco switches and access points, what is Level 15?

5. In previous labs, you were able to configure the access point using Telnet when logged on as Cisco with the password Cisco. In this lab you could not. What changed?

Lab 10.3 Investigating the Cisco Discovery Protocol

Objectives

The Cisco Discovery Protocol (CDP) is a Cisco proprietary, Data Link layer protocol that runs on all Cisco network equipment and is typically enabled on all interfaces by default. CDP reports on directly connected devices only. Each device sends identifying messages and each device monitors the messages sent by other devices. CDP is enabled somewhat differently on wireless access points. It is enabled on the access point's Ethernet port by default, but is only enabled on the access point's radio port if the radio is associated to another wireless infrastructure device, such as an access point or a bridge. Because the access points in your lab are not directly connected to other access points, these other access points will not appear as CDP neighbors of your access point. Information in CDP packets is generally used for network management; however, if it is not necessary on your wireless LAN, you should probably disable CDP. This is because CDP broadcasts information about your network devices. This broadcasting creates overhead as well as a security hole. The purpose of this lab is to become familiar with the types of information available from CDP and to learn how to disable it on an interface. You also will become familiar with the network map feature in the Cisco IOS browser. Unlike CDP, the network map will display all of the access points in the area.

In this lab you will enable the network map feature of the access point, investigate CDP information, disable CDP, and then re-enable it.

After completing this lab, you will be able to:

➤ Describe the network map feature of the Cisco 1200 series access point

➤ Understand the purpose of CDP

➤ Enable and disable CDP

Materials Required

This lab requires the following:

➤ Two laptop computers running Windows XP and configured with a Cisco Aironet adapter

➤ One Cisco Aironet 1200 access point using IOS-based firmware and interface

➤ One UTP patch cable

➤   Power cable for the access point

➤   Access to the wired network through a switch

➤   The access points must be connected via a Cisco switch that has CDP enabled and
    supports access via a Web browser. The switch should be configured for IP, and this
    IP address should be provided to students for this lab.

➤   Completion of the Chapter 2 labs

Estimated completion time: **30 minutes**

LAB ACTIVITY

ACTIVITY

1. Connect and power up your access point if necessary. Turn on your laptops
    and log on.

2. Point to the ADU icon in the tray. Your laptops should be using the Infrastructure
    Mode profile.

3. Open Internet Explorer on one laptop. Browse to your access point using the
    IP address you configured in Lab 2.2. This IP address is listed in Table 2-4. If
    you completed Lab 10.2, you need to log on with one of the new accounts
    because the default administrator account was disabled in that lab.

4. Click **Network Map**. Notice that this feature is disabled by default.

5. Select **Enable** and then click **OK**. Click **Apply**, then click **OK** again to
    enable network mapping. Wait a few seconds and then click the **Refresh** but-
    ton. Do routers and switches display in the network map? _____

    What types of devices display in the network map?

    _____

    Record the names of the devices that are displayed.

    _____

6. Click **Services** and then click **CDP**. Is CDP enabled by default?

    _____

    What is the packet hold time? _____

    CDP packets are sent at intervals of how many seconds? _____

    Scroll down to the CDP Neighbors Table. According to CDP, who is your
    neighbor? _____

    Do the other access points display as neighbors? _____

    Why or why not?

    _____

7. Click the box next to **Capability** for a legend describing the capability codes. What are the capability codes for your neighbor?

   _____

   What do the codes stand for?

   _____

   To what port on the switch is your access point connected? _____

   Close the legend window.

8. Browse to the switch using its IP address. This address will be provided by your instructor. Log on to the switch. Your instructor will give you the necessary username and password to access the system. Click **CDP** at the top of the window. This is functionally the same as telnetting to the switch and using the "show cdp neighbor" command at the command-line interface. The command also works on Cisco routers and access points.

9. Click the IP address of a neighbor and then click **Details** to view additional information regarding the neighbor. Click the **Back** button in the browser to return to the main CDP page.

10. Look at the CDP Options section. Are the default hold time and packet interval the same for the switch as they are for the access points? _____

    Scroll down. Notice that all ports are enabled for CDP by default. As an administrator, you can turn CDP off on any or all of the ports to save bandwidth and provide more security.

11. In the CDP Enabled list box, click the port to which your access point is connected, as recorded in Step 7, and then click **Disable**. Click **Apply**. Your port should appear in the CDP Disabled list box. Figure 10-3 shows CDP disabled on port 20 on a Cisco 1900 series switch. Your interface may look somewhat different.

12. Click your access point's IP address in the Discovered Neighboring Devices list and click the **Browse** button. Log on if prompted. The Web browser interface for your access point should open.

13. Click **Services** and then click **CDP**. Scroll down. By default, your access point lists the switch as a neighbor for the hold-down time of 180 seconds. After 180 seconds, click the **Refresh** button. The switch will eventually be flushed from the neighbor table. Why?

    _____

14. Click the switch browser window, which still should be open. Enable CDP on the port where you disabled it. Make sure your port number appears in the CDP Enabled list before continuing.

15. Close the switch browser window.

16. In the Cisco 1200 access point browser window, click the **Refresh** button until the switch reappears in the neighbor table.

17. Close all windows and shut down the laptops.

10

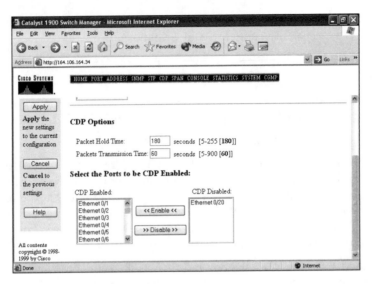

Figure 10-3   CDP options

Certification Objectives

This lab does not map to a certification objective; however, it contains information that will be beneficial to your professional development.

Review Questions

1. What is the purpose of CDP?

2. All Cisco devices run CDP by default. True or False?

3. What is an advantage to using CDP?

4. What are two disadvantages of using CDP?

5. How could the network map feature be used to manage the wireless LAN?

NETWORK SETTINGS AND WIRELESS LAN TROUBLESHOOTING

Labs included in this chapter

➤ Lab 11.1 Troubleshooting Common Wireless LAN Problems

➤ Lab 11.2 Using Link Lights to Troubleshoot the Cisco 1200 Access Point

➤ Lab 11.3 Resetting the Cisco 1200 Access Point

CWNA Exam Objectives	
Objective	Lab
Identify, understand, correct, or compensate for wireless LAN implementation challenges	11.1
Labs 11.2 and 11.3 do not map to a certification objective; however, they contain information that will be beneficial to your professional development.	

LAB 11.1 TROUBLESHOOTING COMMON WIRELESS LAN PROBLEMS

Objectives

Wireless LANs are subject to problems, just as wired networks are. A large part of the role of a wireless network administrator is to solve these problems. Common problems related to wireless networks include multipath, hidden node, near/far, interference, and weather-related issues.

> ➤ Multipath is a received signal made up of the primary signal plus delayed or duplicated signals. It is caused by the reflection of signals off various surfaces such as metal roofs and large bodies of water.

> ➤ Hidden node occurs when two wireless clients cannot hear each other's transmissions because of an obstruction between them. Because they can hear the access point, they transmit at the same time, resulting in excessive collisions.

> ➤ Near/far results from relatively high-power nodes transmitting close to the access point, and relatively low-power nodes transmitting far from the access point. The far clients are drowned out by the noise from the near clients talking to the access point.

> ➤ There are many causes of interference on a wireless LAN. Narrowband interference is RF noise created in a single frequency. All-band interference is noise that is created across the entire spectrum in which your wireless LAN is operating. Co-channel interference is caused by multiple access points in the same physical area configured on the same channel. Adjacent channel interference is caused by multiple access points in the same physical area configured on adjacent channels.

> ➤ Weather does not typically create problems for wireless LANs. Outdoor wireless systems are built to withstand the normal range of weather conditions such as rain, snow, and wind. In some instances, however, weather can cause a problem. A direct lightning strike will destroy your outdoor wireless equipment. Even a nearby lightning strike can damage equipment, which is why lightning arrestors are used with outdoor installations. High winds can move your outdoor antennas and create major network performance degradation until the antennas are realigned. Very dense fog or smog can create a stratification of the air within the fog or smog. When the RF signal goes through these layers of different density, it is bent.

The purpose of this lab is to be able to recognize the meaning of a particular wireless LAN problem and suggest solutions. In this lab you will be presented with six troubleshooting scenarios. You will diagnose the problem and suggest solutions for each scenario.

After completing this lab, you will be able to:

> ➤ Recognize common wireless LAN problems and suggest solutions

Materials Required

This lab requires the following:

➤ Internet access

➤ Pencil or pen

Estimated completion time: **45 minutes**

LAB ACTIVITY

ACTIVITY

Read each scenario and discuss it with your team. Answer the two questions presented after each scenario. Use the Internet and other reference material if you need to search for a definition or other wireless troubleshooting information.

Scenario One: You have 20 wireless LAN users and one access point using the 802.11g standard. Recently, your users have started complaining about decreases in network performance. The complaints are network-wide and not confined to a particular area. You decide to measure background noise on a Sunday when no one is using the wireless LAN. The spectrum analyzer reveals noise across the entire 2.4-GHz spectrum. What type of interference is this?

_____

List two possible solutions to this problem.

_____

_____

Scenario Two: Your company has implemented wireless bridging between two buildings. The access points are indoors and the antennas are outdoors on the roof. Communications between the buildings were fine until a severe thunderstorm occurred a few days ago. Now, you calculate that you are only getting about 10 percent of rated bandwidth. You suspect the storm may be related to your bandwidth problem. The storm produced lightning, heavy rains, and high winds. List two ways the storm may have degraded your wireless network performance.

_____

_____

How will you determine if either of these two possibilities created the problem?

_____

_____

11

Scenario Three: Due to increasing wireless LAN usage, the Dewey, Cheatham, and Howe law firm has recently purchased and installed two additional Cisco 1200 access points. The firm now has three access points, all using the 802.11b standard. Unfortunately, the installation of the two additional access points has resulted in an overall bandwidth decrease for users rather than an increase. You have been hired by the firm to troubleshoot and solve the problem. What do you suspect is the problem and why?

_____

List three possible solutions to this problem.

_____

_____

_____

Scenario Four: You have implemented an 802.11a wireless LAN at your company. Overall, users appear to be satisfied except Veronica and Adrienne, who work in the library. You have tried moving the access point from its location against a column to a position higher up and against the ceiling. In general, the users all noticed an improvement except Veronica and Adrienne. You were going to check the setup on their laptops but changed your mind when they said they have no problems unless they are both in their office and connected to the wireless LAN at the same time. What do you suspect is the problem and why?

_____

List three possible solutions for this problem.

_____

_____

_____

Scenario Five: You have been hired by the Fish Tales restaurant at Smith Mountain Lake to implement an outdoor wireless hot spot for patrons to use while eating outside on the deck, or while dockside on their boats. Upon testing the new wireless system, you notice you are only getting about 20 percent of rated bandwidth at the dockside location. Communications between the deck location and the access point appear to be performing normally. The end of the dock is approximately 150 feet from the access point. Network Stumbler indicates no other wireless LANs in the area. What do you suspect is the problem and why?

_____

List the typical solution for this problem.

_____

Scenario Six: You have been hired by the Dynamite Fertilizer Company to investigate performance-related complaints by some wireless users. You study the wireless site survey that was done by the company's IT Department and conclude that the survey was done correctly, and that all users, regardless of their location in the building, should have consistent and reliable wireless access. You interview the five users who have been complaining and discover there is no problem when they are within 100 feet of the access point, but when they move beyond that distance, communications become unstable and sometimes they cannot associate with the access point. No other users report communications problems, regardless of where they use their wireless devices in the building. What do you suspect and why?

_____

_____

What do you recommend to solve the problem?

_____

Certification Objectives

Objectives for the CWNA exam:

➤ Identify, understand, correct, or compensate for wireless LAN implementation challenges

Review Questions

1. What common problem is caused by reflection off large surfaces such as metal roofs and bodies of water?

2. What problem is caused by an obstruction between users?

3. What problem is caused by multiple access points on the same channel in the same coverage area?

4. What type of interference affects a single frequency?

5. Normal weather typically does not cause a problem for wireless LANs. True or False?

LAB 11.2 USING LINK LIGHTS TO TROUBLESHOOT THE CISCO 1200 ACCESS POINT

Objectives

Almost every networking device has link lights. This includes routers, switches, hubs, and network adapters. Wireless access points typically have link lights as well. In general, green lights indicate operability, amber lights indicate a not-ready status, and a red light almost always means failure. Link lights are very often overlooked as a troubleshooting tool. The purpose of this lab is to investigate the link lights on the Cisco 1200 series access point.

In this lab, you will learn about link light patterns by observing them in various connectivity scenarios.

After completing this lab, you will be able to:

➤ Describe what each link light represents on the Cisco 1200 series access point

➤ Understand what various link light patterns mean

➤ Troubleshoot using link lights

Materials Required

This lab requires the following:

➤ One laptop computer running Windows XP and configured with a Cisco Aironet adapter

➤ One Cisco Aironet 1200 access point using IOS-based firmware and interface

➤ One UTP patch cable

➤ Power cable for the access point

➤ Access to the wired network through a switch

➤ Completion of the Chapter 2 labs

Estimated completion time: **20 minutes**

LAB ACTIVITY

ACTIVITY

1. Shut down your laptops. Unplug your access point and disconnect it from the switch. There should be no wires attached to your access point. The switch should be connected to the wired network and powered up.

2. Study Figure 11-1, which illustrates the relative position of the three link lights on the Cisco 1200 series access point. Notice that the Ethernet link light is closest to the antennas. The status light is in the middle, and the radio light is farthest from the antennas.

NOTE

Although the Cisco Web site might show the link lights in a different order, Figure 11-1 shows them in the correct order.

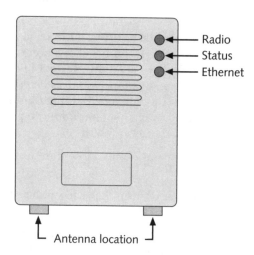

Figure 11-1   Link lights on the Cisco 1200 access point

3. Plug in the power cable and power up the access point, but do not connect the UTP cable. Watch the link light patterns. Notice that the radio and status lights begin flashing green. The Ethernet light becomes amber, which indicates the Ethernet installation test is being performed. Next, all of the lights should turn green and stop flashing. This indicates the IOS is loading. The radio and Ethernet lights should eventually go off, and the status light will blink green. The link lights stabilize in this pattern.

4. Connect the UTP cable from the switch to the Ethernet port on the access point. The Ethernet light begins to blink green. The status light continues to rapidly blink green, which indicates that no clients are associated with the access point. The radio light remains off because no radio signal is being received.

5. Turn on one laptop and log on. Once you are logged on to the system, the radio light on the access point should come on and blink green alternatively with the Ethernet light. The status light should stop blinking because at least one client is associated with the access point. Point to the ADU icon in the tray. A green icon means you are associated with your access point. If you are

not associated, open the Aironet Desktop Utility using the shortcut on the desktop. Click the **Profile Management** tab and double-click your **Infrastructure Mode** profile. Eventually, you should associate with your access point and the status light should stop blinking.

6. Leave the access point powered up but unplug the UTP cable from the Ethernet port on the access point. Both the radio and Ethernet lights should go off, but the status light should still be green and not blinking.

7. Open the Aironet Desktop Utility, if necessary, using the shortcut on the desktop. Click the **Current Status** tab, if necessary. Are you still connected to your access point? _____

8. Click the **Diagnostics** tab. Click the **Troubleshooting** button and then click the **Run Test** button. Watch the radio link light on the access point. It should begin flashing. When the test is finished, click the **View Report** button. Scroll down. Notice that your diagnostics test was successful, as determined by a successful ping of the access point. Even though your laptop has no connectivity to the wired network, everything appears to be fine from the perspective of the client. You still are associated with the access point.

9. Close the Troubleshooting Utility window, but do not close the Aironet Desktop Utility program.

10. Reconnect the UTP cable to the Ethernet port on the access point. The radio and Ethernet lights should begin blinking green.

11. In the Aironet Desktop Utility program, click the **Profile Management** tab. Double-click the **Ad Hoc Mode** profile to activate it. Your ADU icon in the tray should turn gray-white, indicating a loss of connectivity. Your status light will probably begin to blink, but it still may be on and not blinking, indicating your laptop still is associated with it. How is this possible?

_____

12. If your status light is blinking, skip to Step 13. If your status light is not blinking, power down the access point and wait 30 seconds. Power it up again. Watch the link lights as the access point completes its boot cycle. The resulting link light pattern for the three lights should be: Radio–off, Status–blinking green, and Ethernet–blinking green. When you restarted the access point, the association table emptied, so your client is no longer in the table.

13. Double-click the **Infrastructure Mode** profile to activate it. The ADU icon in the tray should turn green to indicate you are again associated with your access point. What is the link light pattern on the access point?

_____

_____

14. Close all programs and shut down the laptop.

Certification Objectives

This lab does not map to a certification objective; however, it contains information that will be beneficial to your professional development.

Review Questions

1. List in order the link lights on the Cisco 1200 access point. Begin with the light closest to the antennas.

2. What link light pattern would you expect to see if wireless users were associated with the access point and surfing the Web?

3. What should you check if both the radio and Ethernet lights are off but the status light is green?

11

4. It is possible for wireless clients to have no connectivity to the wireless network when the link light pattern indicates all is well. True or False?

5. In general, what do red lights, amber lights, and green lights indicate on wireless devices?

LAB 11.3 RESETTING THE CISCO 1200 ACCESS POINT

Objectives

At some point, you may want or need to reset the access point to the factory defaults. One common reason for a reset is that users forget the logins and passwords that have been configured on the access point, thereby preventing access to it. Another common reason is a complicated configuration that isn't working. Often it is faster to reset the device and start over, rather than trying to reconfigure it one command at a time. There are basically two ways to do a reset, and both produce the same result with one minor exception. Using the Web browser interface to reset the access point will not reset static IP addresses that have been configured. This is so you can remain connected to the access point using this address. Using the mode button on the access point will reset it to obtain IP addresses automatically. You may be familiar with the Cisco erase start command, which is used to reset completely

Cisco router configurations. While this command works on the 1200 series access point, it does not completely reset the configuration. For example, in addition to IP addresses not being reset, access lists and some other parameters remain configured after the erase start command is issued on the access point. The purpose of this lab is to reset the access point using both the Web browser method and the mode button method, and then to compare the results.

In this lab you will reset the access point using the Web browser interface and investigate the results. Then, you will do a hard reset using the mode button on the access point and re-establish connectivity using the default profile.

After completing this lab, you will be able to:

➤ Do a soft reset on the Cisco 1200 series access point

➤ Do a hard reset on the Cisco 1200 series access point

Materials Required

This lab requires the following:

➤ Two laptop computers running Windows XP and configured with a Cisco Aironet adapter

➤ One Cisco Aironet 1200 access point using IOS-based firmware and interface

➤ One UTP patch cable

➤ Power cable for the access point

➤ Access to the wired network through a switch

➤ Completion of the Chapter 2 labs

Estimated completion time: **30 minutes**

LAB ACTIVITY

ACTIVITY

1. Connect and power up your access point if necessary. Turn on your laptops and log on. Point to the ADU icon in the tray. Your laptops should be using the Infrastructure Mode profile.

2. On one laptop, open Internet Explorer. Browse to your access point using the IP address you configured in Lab 2.2. This IP address is listed in Table 2-4. If you completed Lab 10.2, you will need to log on with one of the new accounts because the default administrator account was disabled in that lab. Make sure that pop-up blocking is disabled in your browser before continuing with the lab.

3. Click **System Software** and then click **System Configuration**.

4. Click the **Reset to Defaults** button. At this point, various warning windows might appear, depending on the browser, plug-ins, and other software installed on the computer. Click **OK**.

5. When you see a System Restarting Now window, close it. Watch the link lights on your access point as the system is restarted. You will lose your connection because the Infrastructure Mode profile on your laptop does not match the default profile on the access point.

6. Attach a DB-9-to-RJ-45 adapter to the COM1 port on the back of the laptop. Connect a rollover cable to the DB-9 connector. Attach the other end of the cable to the console port on the back of your team's access point.

7. Click **Start**, point to **All Programs**, point to **Accessories**, point to **Communications**, point to **HyperTerminal**, and then click the connection you created in Lab 2.2. If you didn't save your connection, you must create a new one. Follow Steps 6 through 8 of Lab 2.2 to create a new connection.

8. Text appears in the HyperTerminal window. If text does not appear, press **Enter**. Eventually, the ap> prompt displays. Has the name of the access point been reset? _____

9. Type **enable** and press **Enter**. You are prompted for a password. You no longer have to log on as a specific user because the access point has been reset. The default password is Cisco, and it is case sensitive. Type **Cisco** and press **Enter**. Notice that the prompt changes to ap#.

10. Type **show run** and press **Enter**. The current configuration of the access point displays. Have the users you created in a previous lab been removed from the configuration? _____

11. Press the Spacebar and scroll through the output as necessary. What is the name of your SSID? _____

   Is this the default SSID? _____

12. What is the IP address on the BVI1 interface? _____

   Did that IP address reset to the factory default? _____

13. Now you will do a hard reset on the access point using the mode button. Do not close the HyperTerminal program or disconnect the console cable. Disconnect the power from the access point. Press and hold down the mode button while you reconnect the power to the access point. The mode button should be next to the console port on the access point. Hold down the mode button for a moment or so until the status link light (the light in the middle) turns amber.

14. In a minute or so, all three lights on the access point should turn green, indicating that the IOS is loading. Return to the HyperTerminal window and watch while the system loads.

15. Wait until the system stops loading, then press **Enter** to get to the ap> prompt. Enter the **enable** command and then enter **Cisco** when prompted for a password.

16. Enter the **show run** command and use the Spacebar to scroll down to the BVI1 interface area of the configuration. How will the IP address on the BVI1 be configured?

_____

17. Close HyperTerminal. Click **Yes** when the warning window appears.

18. On both laptops, open the Aironet Desktop Utility by double-clicking the desktop shortcut.

19. Click the **Profile Management** tab and double-click the **Default** profile. You should reconnect to the access point, as this profile is designed to work with the access point as is (out of the box). Because you just performed a hard reset on the access point, it should be back to its out-of-the-box configuration.

20. Close all windows and shut down the laptops. Disconnect the console cable.

Certification Objectives

This lab does not map to a certification objective; however, it contains information that will be beneficial to your professional development.

Review Questions

1. Name two common reasons for resetting an access point.

2. Why doesn't the Web browser reset method reset the IP address on the BVI1 interface?

3. List the steps to perform a hard reset on the Cisco 1200 series access point.

4. The erase start command is essentially the same as a reset on the Cisco 1200 series access point. True or False?

5. Which reset method do you prefer and why?

PERSONAL, METROPOLITAN, AND WIDE AREA WIRELESS NETWORKS

Labs included in this chapter

➤ Lab 12.1 Investigating ZigBee (802.15.4)
➤ Lab 12.2 Comparing Broadband Wireless Systems
➤ Lab 12.3 Exploring the Future of Wireless

CWNA Exam Objectives	
Objective	**Lab**
Identify some of the different uses for spread spectrum technologies	12.1, 12.2
Lab 12.3 does not map to a certification objective; however, it contains information that will be beneficial to your professional development.	

LAB 12.1 INVESTIGATING ZIGBEE (802.15.4)

Objectives

Most of us associate personal area networks with the Bluetooth technology and with the 802.15 standard, probably because the first version of 802.15, designated as 802.15.1, was based on the Bluetooth standard. The 802.15.4 standard was ratified in 2003, and it specifies personal area networking technologies. One proprietary technology based on the 802.15.4 standard is ZigBee. Technically speaking, the IEEE 802.15.4 standard refers only to the Physical layer and MAC sublayer of the OSI model, as most IEEE 802.x standards do. ZigBee builds on the IEEE standard at the Data Link layer and extends it up through layers 3 and 4. The objective of this lab is to help you become familiar with this latest wireless personal area network standard.

In this lab, you will investigate ZigBee using Internet Explorer and the Wikipedia Web site.

After completing this lab, you will be able to:

➤ Describe the latest wireless personal area network technology known as ZigBee

Materials Required

This lab requires the following:

➤ Internet access

➤ Pencil or pen

Estimated completion time: **20 minutes**

This lab depends on a Web site that may have changed slightly since the time of this writing.

NOTE

ACTIVITY

LAB ACTIVITY

1. Open Internet Explorer and browse to *www.wikipedia.org*. Click **English**. In the search text box, type **zigbee** and then click the **Go** button.

2. List some uses for ZigBee technology.

   _____

3. With respect to power consumption, how do ZigBee devices compare with other wireless devices?

   _____

4. List the three types of ZigBee devices from most to least expensive.

5. Describe a ZigBee coordinator.

6. Describe a ZigBee FFD.

7. Describe a ZigBee RFD.

8. What is the physical topology of a ZigBee network?

9. Is a ZigBee network infrastructure mode-based or ad hoc mode-based?

10. What are the three unlicensed bands used by ZigBee?

11. What is the maximum rated bandwidth for any ZigBee system?

12. What is the maximum transmission range for any ZigBee system?

13. Close your browser.

12

Certification Objectives

Objectives for the CWNA exam:

➤ Identify some of the different uses for spread spectrum technologies

Review Questions

1. Bluetooth and ZigBee are both wireless personal area network technologies. True or False?

2. What are two advantages of ZigBee over Bluetooth?

3. Every ZigBee network may have one or more coordinators. True or False?

4. Non-beaconing ZigBee networks consume less power. True or False?

5. What is the difference between ZigBee and 802.15.4?

LAB 12.2 COMPARING BROADBAND WIRELESS SYSTEMS

Objectives

There is a developing market for communicating wirelessly at DSL and cable speeds over a wide area (WWAN), just as users do on LANs. The 802.11 equipment can be used outdoors, but there are several problems with it being used to deliver what is known as broadband wireless access (BWA). First, 802.11 does not do a good job of providing guaranteed bandwidth for a relatively large number of users. In addition, the 802.11 standard uses unlicensed frequency bands, which can become quite congested and interference-ridden. To address the challenge of BWA, the IEEE has created two standards: 802.16e and 802.20. The 802.16e standard is based on the 802.16a standard known as WiMAX. The 802.16e standard adds mobility to the original fixed wireless standard. The 802.20 standard is brand new, and sometimes is referred to as Mobile Broadband Wireless Access (MBWA). Unlike 802.11, the IEEE BWA standards do not use carrier sensing mechanisms at the MAC sublayer. Rather, they use a form of multiplexing, either TDMA or CDMA. Many in the industry wonder why the IEEE has sanctioned two BWA standards that, in terms of the wireless market, appear to be competing with each other. In addition, MBWA may be positioning itself as a direct competitor to 3G networks, which is the next generation of mobile digital wireless technologies. 3G supports packet switching, wireless broadband multimedia, and global roaming. At the time of this writing, MBWA connectivity has been verified at vehicular speeds of 155 mph. The highest verified vehicular speed for WiMAX is 93 mph. WiMAX may have the advantage, though, as the 802.16 standard is well-known and is working to become interoperable with Korea's WiBro and Europe's HIPERMAN standards.

In this lab, you will investigate and compare these IEEE BWA standards using Internet Explorer and the Wi-Fi Planet Web site.

After completing this lab, you will be able to:

➤ Better understand broadband wireless

➤ Explain the differences and similarities between 802.16e and 802.20

Materials Required

This lab requires the following:

➤ Internet access

➤ Pen or pencil

Estimated completion time: **20 minutes**

ACTIVITY

1. Open Internet Explorer and browse to *www.wi-fiplanet.com*. In the search text box, type **802.16e vs. 802.20** and click **Go**. Click the **802.16e vs. 802.20** link to open the document. If this Web site has changed and the article is no longer available, modify your search to find the required information.

2. The left column of Table 12-1 contains features of broadband wireless service. Match each feature to the correct IEEE specification by writing "802.16e" or "802.20" in the right column. You may believe the feature being described is part of both specifications or neither specification. If so, write "Both" or "None," respectively. Use the article you browsed for help.

Table 12-1   802.16e versus 802.20

Feature	IEEE Specification
Supports vehicular speeds up to 155 mph	
Designed for widespread deployment like a cellular network	
Supplies broadband wireless access	
Uses the 2- to 6-GHz licensed frequency bands	
Allows for mobility	
Has a maximum documented vehicular speed of 93 mph	
Will probably be the first to hit the market	
A direct competitor to 3G wireless cellular technology	
Targets mobile PDAs and laptops	
Targets high-speed mobility	
Can be implemented using 802.11 equipment	
Designed to be deployed in an existing wireless footprint	
Sometimes is referred to as the wireless MAN standard	
Uses licensed frequency bands below 3.5 GHz	

3. Close your browser.

Certification Objectives

Objectives for the CWNA exam:

➤ Identify some of the different uses for spread spectrum technologies

Review Questions

1. What is the problem with using 802.11 to provide users with broadband wireless access?

2. What is 802.16a called?

3. What is 802.20 called?

4. The IEEE broadband wireless access standards are based on CSMA/CA. True or False?

5. What is Europe's broadband wireless access standard called?

LAB 12.3 EXPLORING THE FUTURE OF WIRELESS

Objectives

The IEEE is aggressively involved in developing wireless standards, as demonstrated by the sheer number of 802.11 working groups that have been organized. Wireless working group are defined by a letter that is added to 802.11; this letter is associated with a particular task assigned to the working group. Many of these working groups might produce an 802.11 standard, which will be designated by the letter. Most of us now are familiar with 802.11g and 802.11i. At one time, these were working groups that developed a standard, which now is in use. However, not every working group produces a standard. Some working groups fade away, some switch to another task, and some join together to form another working group Currently, the IEEE is working on several new projects identified as 802.11d, 802.11 802.11h, 802.11j, 802.11k, 802.11n, 802.11r, and 802.11s.

In this lab, you will navigate to *www.techworld.com* and explore these latest 802.11 standards

After completing this lab, you will be able to:

➤ Describe the most recent 802.11 standards

Materials Required

This lab requires the following:

➤ Internet access

➤ Pen or pencil

Estimated completion time: **20 minutes**

ACTIVITY

1. Open Internet Explorer and browse to *www.techworld.com*. In the search text box, type **802.11 alphabet soup** and click **Go**. Click the **Features** link in the right column, then click **Keep track of the 802.11 alphabet soup** to open the document. If this Web site has changed and the article is no longer available, modify your search to find the required information.

2. The left column of Table 12-2 contains definitions of the latest IEEE 802.11 standards. Match each definition to the correct IEEE specification by writing the specification (for example, 802.11d) in the right column. Use the article you browsed for help.

12

Table 12-2 IEEE wireless standards

Definition	IEEE Specification
A wireless roaming standard that is a recommended practice rather than a formal standard	
Implements routing on access points, allowing them to forward traffic to other access points	
Creates a way for users to roam without reauthenticating at each new access point	
Allows access points and wireless clients to avoid interfering with communications in the same 5-GHz frequency band	
Allows access points to broadcast a country code with specific rules so clients can connect with any open wireless LAN, regardless of country	
Manages radio resources by standardizing radio measurements related to roaming, channel use, and client devices	
Involves the use of the 4.9- to 5-GHz frequency band, which was recently allocated for homeland security in the U.S.	
High-throughput standard that supports data rates of at least 100 Mbps in the 2.4-GHz frequency band	

3. Close your browser.

Certification Objectives

This lab does not map to a certification objective; however, it contains information that will be beneficial to your professional development.

Review Questions

1. How is an IEEE working group identified?

2. Not all IEEE working groups produce a standard. True or False?

3. What recently completed 802.11 standard claims to fix many of the security weaknesses associated with 802.11?

4. What industry trade group certifies and promotes 802.11-based products?

5. What does MIMO stand for and how is it related to 802.11n?

A

LAB PREPARATIONS AND TIPS FOR SUCCESS IN THE CLASSROOM

This appendix provides instructions and tips for a successful hands-on wireless course using this lab manual. This appendix includes instructions for required equipment, student teams, laptop preparation, additional software, access point preparation, naming conventions, and lab exercises. Also, Figure A-1 shows the physical layout of the equipment during a typical lab. Setup information for the Linksys routers is not included because students set up and configure these routers during the labs. Depending on how you purchase the Cisco 1200 series access points, these devices also may be ready to use out of the box.

Equipment Required

For a class of 20, I recommend the following list of equipment:

- Twelve laptops with an Ethernet connection, a CD-ROM drive, and a Type II PC slot for a wireless adapter
- Twelve Cisco Aironet 802.11a/b/g cardbus wireless LAN client adapters with drivers and utilities software
- Six Cisco 1200 series access points with IOS interface (not VxWorks) and preferably with a "G" radio
- Six Linksys wireless "G" routers (model WRT54G preferred)
- One Cisco switch (1900 series or higher)
- Seven UTP patch cables
- One patch cable or crossover cable to connect the switch to the campus network
- Six console cables
- Six DB-9-to-RJ-45 adapters if necessary
- Appropriate power cables for all devices

Student Teams

The labs in this lab manual are designed to be completed by students working in teams. For a class of 20, I recommend five teams of four students. If there are fewer than 20 students in the class, you can make adjustments, but try not to have more than four students per team. Each team will be assigned two laptops, one Cisco 1200 series access point, and one Linksy wireless router. The instructor also will have an access point, a wireless router, and two laptops in order to practice the labs in advance, if necessary. In addition, a few labs require the use of instructor equipment.

Laptop Preparation

You need to purchase your laptops with an Ethernet NIC installed, a CD-ROM drive, and a Type II PC slot for a wireless adapter. The laptops may come with an internal wireless card already installed, but that connection will not be used. Instead, students will install and configure a Cisco Aironet 802.11a/b/g cardbus wireless adapter. These adapters come with a CD that contains the drivers and utilities. Instructors should not install the adapters or the drivers and utilities, because the students will learn to perform this important activity in the Chapter 2 labs. You will need to install Windows XP with Service Pack 2 on the laptop

I highly recommend creating an image so the laptops can be easily restored before the next group of students begins working on them. This lab manual assumes the following Windows XP configuration:

- IP configuration obtained via DHCP (except on instructor laptops)
- Laptops named using the naming conventions described later in this appendix
- Control Panel configured for Category View
- Windows XP firewall turned off
- Automatic update notification turned off after the latest updates have been installed
- Winzip software installed
- Antivirus software installed (optional)
- Logon as administrator with no password
- Disabled internal wireless connection if there is one

Additional Software

Some of the labs require additional software, all of which is free. While the lab exercises provide instructions for downloading any necessary software, you may want to download all of the software to a CD and make copies for your students. Alternatively, you could make the downloaded software part of the laptop image. Either method will ensure that the correct version of the software is available if a Web site has changed since the lab was written. The following is a list of additional software:

- AiroPeek SE (not NX)
- AirMagnet Laptop Demo
- Network Stumbler
- 3CS117.zip FTP program
- Putty.exe
- Tournament.ssf (This is a big file used to determine throughput. You can use any file that is about 75 MB, as long as you rename it tournament.ssf.)

Cisco 1200 Series Access Point

You should attempt to purchase your access points with the "G" radio already installed and with an IOS rather than the VxWorks interface. The IOS commands such as the ones used on Cisco routers and switches are not available with the VxWorks interface. When I purchased my access points, they came with an 802.11b radio installed and were configured with VxWorks. I had to upgrade from VxWorks to the IOS firmware, then upgrade from the 802.11a/b firmware to the 802.11a/b/g firmware, and then physically replace the "B" radio with a "G" radio. While this wasn't difficult, it can be avoided by ordering the correct equipment.

The firmware image (IOS) loaded on your access points is very important. This lab manual is based on the c1200-k9w7-tar.122-15.JA.tar (release name 12.2.15-JA) firmware image. There have been two upgrades since I began writing this lab manual. The first was dated 2004-09 and named c1200-k9w7-tar.122-15.XR2.tar (release name 12.2.15-XR2). This upgrade has been tested with this lab manual and is compatible with every lab. However, the most recent image, named c1200-k9w7-tar.123-4.JA.tar (release name 12.3.4-JA), is not 100 percent compatible with this lab manual. I highly recommend that you do not use this image or any newer image. The newer image involves some security changes that may affect some labs in this manual:

- No default SSID

- SSID broadcasting disabled

- IOS boots with radio interface shut down

If you are an experienced user of the 1200 series, you can probably overcome any inconsistencies between the latest firmware and the lab manual instructions. Still, I recommend using one of the compatible firmware images.

Other than making sure your access points are using the IOS interface and that the firmware image is a correct version, nothing else is required for class use. The students will perform all the necessary configuration during the lab exercises.

In Lab 2.2, you will need to provide students with an IP address, subnet mask, and default gateway for their Cisco 1200 series access point. You also will need this configuration information for your access point. It is best to get these static IP addresses from your network administrator before you begin the course. I also find it helpful to configure my instructor laptops with static IP information because in a few labs, the students connect to those laptops.

In Chapter 11, the students reset the access points so they are ready for the next group of students. You will have to reset the Linksys wireless routers.

Naming Conventions

The lab manual is written with the assumption that equipment will be named using the Department of Defense (DOD) phonetic alphabet. So, if you have 12 laptops, you will name them alpha, bravo, charlie, delta, echo, foxtrot, golf, hotel, india, juliet, kilo, and lima. Kilo and lima are the instructor laptops. If you are using less than 12 laptops, I suggest that you still use the names kilo and lima for the instructor laptops, to be consistent with lab manual instructions. The laptops should be named when you install Windows XP. Obviously, if you download an image to the laptops, they will all have the same name and you will have to rename all but one of them.

Access points and Linksys routers also are named, but students provide these names as part of the lab exercises. Team names, access point names, and Linksys wireless router names are simply a combination of laptop names. So, for example, the first team is alpha-bravo, the second team is charlie-delta, and so forth. The alpha-bravo team has a Cisco 1200 series access point and a Linksys router that they will name alpha-bravo, and their two laptops will be named alpha and bravo. The instructor's access point and wireless router are named kilo-lima. All equipment should be labeled with the names to help students keep track of their team's equipment. It helps if all the laptops are stored in a locked, mobile cart in which they can be plugged in and charged before class. I usually charge the laptops during the lecture portion of the class so they are ready for lab use without power cords.

The general physical layout of the lab is shown in Figure A-1. This figure reflects the layout most often used to complete the labs in this manual. A few of the labs require a slightly different layout. These variations are noted in figures and instructions throughout the lab manual and in the lab solutions files as necessary.

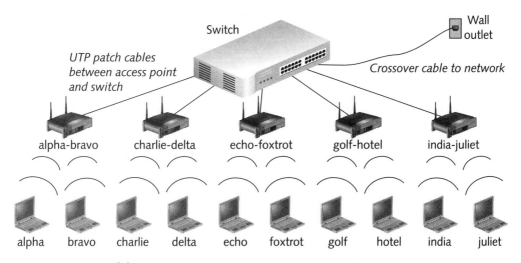

Figure A-1   Basic lab setup

Lab Exercises

The Chapter 2 labs are crucial to all other labs in the manual that involve wirele
connectivity and the Cisco 1200 series access points. In this chapter, students install th
Cisco Aironet wireless client adapter in the laptops, configure the drivers, and use th
utilities to connect to their access point. They also configure their access point for basic la
use. Lab 3.4 is crucial for all other Linksys wireless router labs, as the initial setup an
configuration for the device is done in this lab. After the Chapter 2 labs and Lab 3.4 ar
complete, the instructor can pick and choose which labs the students will perform. Only on
or two labs depend on a previous lab other than the Chapter 2 labs and Lab 3.4. It
important, however, that students do labs in the order presented; for example, Lab 8.4 shoul
not be done before Lab 7.1 or Lab 8.3.

Students can answer the review questions at the end of each lab based on the lab itself. Man
of the answers can be found in the Objectives section of the lab. The instructor manu.
contains the answers to the activity questions and the review questions. Helpful notes for la
success also are included where necessary.